Gladys Bingham
September 1920

ADVENTURES IN COMMON SENSE

BY DR. FRANK CRANE
AUTHOR OF "JUST HUMAN,"
"FOOTNOTES TO LIFE,"
"WAR AND WORLD GOVERNMENT," ETC.

NEW YORK: JOHN LANE COMPANY
LONDON: JOHN LANE, THE BODLEY HEAD, MCMXVIII

Second Edition

TO

JOHN H. PATTERSON

OF DAYTON

THIS BOOK IS RESPECTFULLY DEDICATED
IN RECOGNITION OF A HELPFUL FRIENDSHIP

CONTENTS

ADVENTURES IN COMMON SENSE

BY WAY OF INTRODUCTION I TELL MY OWN ADVENTURE IN COMMON SENSE

In 1909 I was pastor of the Union Congregational Church at Worcester, Massachusetts.

It was a strong Church. My relations with the people were delightful. My salary was good, as preachers' salaries go. I was practically settled for life, as a New England Church rarely dismisses its pastor.

In the midst of this comfortable career I suddenly resigned. For these reasons:

My position was too secure. It was not precarious enough. Unless one is a bit uncertain where his daily bread is coming from he lacks the atmosphere of hazard necessary if one is to keep young. I was drifting into the horrible stagnation of the endowed class. I was forty-eight. I wanted to get out into the arena and wrestle with men, else I felt that my mental and spiritual muscles would stiffen. I longed to hunt for work, and was tired of having employment assured me.

In other words I wanted Adventure. I wanted the Open Road, and was tired of the House.

There was no friction with my people. I loved

them and they gave every indication of liking me.

I had no theological or credal difficulties. My church allowed me entire intellectual freedom; in fact, they were as progressive and independent in thought as I.

And there was a deeper reason for my stepping out of a regular pulpit. No matter how excellent a congregation may be, it is limited; the very word "Church" means "called out," and implies exclusiveness. But in me there had grown a passion for the multitude. I realized that my Maker had intended me for an Outsider. All the while that I sat in my study or stood in my pulpit I was yearning for the great, unherded mass of men and women who never came to my Church, many of them to no Church at all. Those were my people. My message was to them, not to the elect.

I do not want to be taken as criticizing the Church. I am persuaded it is the best place for most preachers to work. All I say is that my feeling forced me out into the highway and market.

It took me forty-eight years to come to myself, but finally I found out where I belonged.

So I said to my wife: "I want to quit. I want to get out and play with the boys in the alley. Above all I want to write for the Newspapers. Of course, preaching is all I know, but I believe the best place to preach is in the columns of the daily press. Jesus was not in the Temple; He was by the roadside; He went down to where humanity was and talked there. I want to try that once before I die.

"Our children are now grown up and through school. We are foot-loose. Let us take to the open, and see what happens."

The idea appealed to her. I resigned. I had no money. Preachers rarely save money. So I borrowed $1,600 on my life insurance, and we began our wanderings by going by water to Chicago, up the Hudson, down the St. Lawrence, and through the Great Lakes.

I began to infest the Chicago Newspapers. I found out that while I desired to write for the newspapers I was quite alone in my desire. The editors laughed at me. "Why," they said, "we can get preaching stuff by the yard—for nothing. Nobody reads it. We want news."

I argued with them. "You are mistaken. Human nature is the same as it has always been, and people have always liked to be preached to. The only trouble is that nobody has offered preaching of the right kind to the newspapers. Mine is the right kind. Try it."

At last Leigh Reilly, then editor of the *Chicago Evening Post,* fell. He accepted my proposal to run a stickful or two on his editorial page, under the title, "The Philosopher's Corner." For this I received one dollar a day, but that was nothing compared to the immense bliss and rapture I received from seeing my pet notion exploited at last. I never expect to be as happy again as I was at seeing my name in the *Post.*

It is pleasant to feel the response of an audience to the spoken word, and this is the spiritual reward of the public speaker. But I now tasted the delight of seeing my writing in print, and the joy of it was more than that of the orator.

About six months I lasted on the *Post,* at that time the high-brow paper of Chicago. Then the owner fired me, fearing probably that there must be something shady about any man that had quit preaching. An ex-preacher is a suspicious character, I discovered. The average mind reasons: "There must have been something wrong or he would not have left the pulpit." If he left a good salary also, the suspicion hardens to a certainty. I suppose that the proprietor feared that if I should suddenly get drunk, or run off with my neighbor's wife, or do some other ex-ministerial high-jinks, the elegant and refined readers of the *Post* would be down on him for carrying my name on his pages.

Anyway, I was gently dismissed, though Reilly assured me that he, and all the boys around the office, liked the stuff.

Meanwhile, however, I had received a letter from Edward Bok, of the *Ladies' Home Journal,* enclosing a clipping from my Philosopher's Corner in the *Post,* and asking me whether I did that just once, by accident, or whether I could do it again, and regularly. I sat down and wrote him twenty little articles of the kind he had noticed, and sent them to him and said that the best way to answer his question was to submit specimens.

For the benefit of struggling young authors, seeking for the key to success, I may state a curious element of this correspondence. Each of my twenty articles was on a separate sheet. Some of the sheets were pink and some white. Mr. Bok accepted all those that were pink. This ranks about on a par with most hints to aspiring authors.

Mr. Bok ran a page of my matter for several months. I had also broken into the *Chicago Tribune,* and George Matthew Adams was using a daily brief article in his syndicate. The Hearst papers were buying some at my counter.

I was now feeling so rich that I went to Europe and spent a year or so living in Rome, Paris and London, talking with common folks and learning their philosophy.

The syndicate of The Associated Newspapers was formed about this time, consisting of some forty newspapers throughout the United States and Canada, and I became a writer for them, a position I yet hold.

My experiment has succeeded. I will tell why.

At first I asked a literary friend to write this introduction. He replied, "I will do so with pleasure. But why don't you do it yourself? What I would write would be only the usual appreciation of one author by another, and would interest readers but slightly. Tell your story yourself and people will read it. You know more about yourself than any one else knows."

Hence this blurb.

Why have I succeeded in getting people to read my articles and inducing newspapers to pay for them?

My opinion has changed. It now seems to me that it is not so much the Sermon people want, as it is the Essay.

The Essay had finally achieved the distinction of being praised by all and read by none. It had become a highly developed literary ornament. A few persons in Boston, and a few Brahmans elsewhere, read Essays. The vast commons, never.

The first thing I did to the Essay was to make it short. I perceived that the average intelligence wanted one point, not a dozen. A man will seize one idea and devour it with relish; overload his plate and you kill his appetite.

People like ideas, but they like them *à la carte* and not *table d'hôte*.

The old-fashioned Essay was a conglomerate of many ideas. *Wer zu viel will geht oft leer aus.*

I took one point, sharpened it and drove it home. I resisted the ecclesiastical temptation to firstly and tenthly. As a result, the reader, first seeing that it wasn't very long, tackled it. He remembered it. He was tempted to cut it out and carry it in his pocketbook.

Second, I realized that the most interesting things in the world are the old things and the common things. Hence I did not strain after the outlandish and the unusual, in the selection of themes, but went into the living-room, bed-room and kitchen of the human heart, and spoke of what I saw there. I tried to tell the housewife what a wonderful thing her work-basket is, and how it is related to the spheres and to her everlasting soul; to show the cook the divine relation of dishwashing to life; to make the business man see the River of God running through his office; and to reveal to the shop girl that her tears and laughter are just as real and as rich in human quality as the emotions of duchesses and famous actresses.

I found among the undistinguished and the unelect a mine of human gold.

Furthermore I did not take my wares to the kings and nobles of literature, to the stately Quarterlies and other magazines that give tone to the library table but lie uncut and unread. Having stuff for the millions I went with it to the newspapers, which the millions read. Having a passion for democracy I took the greatest of all democratic vehicles, the newspaper, which is read by millionaire and hobo, fat and rich gentlemen and lean and hungry, fine ladies and servant girls, read by the President and by the peddler.

I found that the same ideas that are preached from pulpits to the chosen few, and lectured on by professors to select classes, and favored by intellectuals generally, are equally welcomed by common folks, only they want it unaffected and disinfected. They, too, love problems of conscience and conduct, of God and destiny, of love and mystery. They do not, however, care for literary posing, for the antics of conventional culture, nor for the conceit of technical phraseology.

Hence I once for all renounced all ambition toward fine writing. I tried to say my say in the clearest, fewest words possible. I went straight at my point and quit when I had got done.

I found out that when one writes simply and only to be understood, in entire disregard of rules of art, without stumbling over his medium, one writes entertainingly.

I have taken the dead Essay and made it a living thing. I have taken the Essay out of its glass coffin in the library and put it on the office desk, on the woman's work-table, and in the laborer's pocket.

This I have done without using the ready-made platform of the preacher, the prestige of a famous name, the antics of the mountebank or the salacity of the border-bands of literature.

My name meant nothing to readers. What I said was read for its own sake.

To sum up, my conviction was and is that the Short Idea, or Essay, can be made as interesting as the Short Story. This I did, because I believed it; this I believe, because I did it.

I do not know whether these Essays are good literature or not. Only to-day they are asked for, paid for and read. To-morrow the critics will tell you why. Also they will tell you why they should not have succeeded.

All I do here is to tell you why and how they were written. I ought to know, for I wrote them myself.

At any rate, here is a bookful of them, and the gentle reader may judge for himself.

FRANK CRANE

THE SMILE OF LA JOCONDE

WHEN Leonardo's Mona Lisa finally got back to her place upon the walls of the Louvre all the world came to see her—at least on the first day of her home-coming some twenty thousand trooped by to have a look at the most famous of paintings.

And there, with those placid hands upon her lap, she sat in her frame, regarding the passers-by with her amused and superior smile, very much as you would look upon the antics of your pet kitten.

"Why worry?" she seemed to say. "Here I am, as you see. I came back, of course, since it is written. It was destiny. All of us but follow our programme. I am the original predestinarian. I am the cheerful fatalist. Men and women struggle and fume, but always by and by they do what is set down for them to do, in the book of fate. It is to smile!

"I am the companion of Omar Khayyam. For I am the Looker-On. I do not mingle with the energies of men. I am the Bystander.

"My Maker was the Many-Minded One. He was a Philosopher. Philosophy is aloofness. I am the daughter of the Aloof. Leonardo smiled at men in his heart, and made me that I might smile at them forever.

"I am the Eternal Feminine. I do not labor. I sit. I judge. I smile.

"I know, hence I am amused. I am in the secret of things, and that is always rather funny; it is so different from the appearance of things.

"In the core of wisdom is laughter. In the secret springs of history there is grim humor. Underneath the intense activities, the fierce rivalries, the burning passions of men, back of the debates of senates, the thunder of wars, the display of wealth, and the earnestness of reformers, there is something that makes me smile. I cannot tell you what it is. You would have to be a Leonardo to understand.

"Wisdom is Jocund as it nears Perfection. God is Glad.

"This at least I can hint to you. You are fretting over nothing at all. The universe is Kind. It means well by man. When you get through with life, and pass through revealing death, and see what it all means, the first thing you will do will be to have a good laugh.

"Tragedy is the greatest of humbugs. I have peeped behind the veil. I know that every Jack will have his Jill, every wrong be righted, and the Short Story called Life will have a happy ending.

"I have seen the end of the world. It is pleasant. That is why all through the Revolution and

Tyranny, the flow and ebb of progress, Louis the Luxurious, and Robespierre the Terrible, I have sat so contented and unruffled.

"I smiled to see how long it took men to discover Gravitation, Steam, Electricity, Evolution, Democracy. The race is so stupid, so awkward, and amusing.

"I am Nature. Look at me and you see how self-satisfied and smiling Nature goes about her business.

"I am Mankind, playing, procreating, joking, planting trees, building houses, and going away.

"I am Death, which is the most delightful surprise, and not at all the horrible catastrophe you fancy.

"I am Everything and Everybody. Some things and some people are morbid and vicious, but, in the All, cheer predominates.

"I am in the Secret of God, and the Secret of God is—a smile.

"Men take themselves so seriously. They think they do things. In reality they are leaves upon the streams, clouds in the sky, motes in the sunbeam. They are but chess-men. He who moves is God, who smiles.

"I am the Soul of kittens that play with their tails, of puppies that frisk, of little lambs that gambol, of all things newborn. I am Youth forever recurrent.

"If I could speak I should utter the greatest words ever spoken, and recall to you that the world's Master said: 'I am the Resurrection and the Life.' "

It is said that the crowd that viewed Mona Lisa that day were of "a light gayety, with a decided tendency to crack jokes." Even the police guarding her were smiling.

The incomparable Leonardo, full of strange and cunning secrets, embodied his whole wisdom in a Smile, that it might infect the world.

A RECIPE FOR HAPPINESS

It is worth while to try any recipe for happiness.

Here is one that at least is to be commended for its simplicity and for the fact that it is within the reach of all.

It is to rid yourself of your notion of your RIGHTS.

Think a bit, and you will see that the greater part of all the indignities, chagrins, and humiliations you have had to endure arise from certain ideas you entertain about what is DUE you.

If you can knead your mind about until you come to the conclusion that NOTHING AT ALL is due you, happiness is pretty sure to come in and take permanent lodgings in your heart.

Most of us have a contempt for manipulating our minds to suit the inevitable, and an admiration for those of us who can coerce events to suit their desires.

But, for instance, suppose, when you awake in the morning, before you get out of bed to do your gymnastics, you do a little mental exercise. Ask yourself: "Why should any one love me? Why should I be sought, admired, or praised? What right have I to health or wealth? Others suffer, why should I be happy? I have no claims on the universe, so if anything good comes my way to-day I shall consider myself in luck."

Before you get up clean out of your mind every feeling of your RIGHTS, and see what kind of a day you will have.

Don't try for more than one day, at first, for it will tax your forces.

Old habits of thought will bring constant suggestions, that you are being abused, imposed upon, oppressed and devoured. Be patient. Put these ideas away. Try, just one day, to act on the theory that you have no rights at all.

Expect no gratitude when you help the poor. Look for no recognition when you accommodate a friend. Give up your seat in the crowded car. Step back and wait for others at the theatre box office. Require no attention from your servants, your children, or your wife. Be a door-mat—it's only for one day.

By night you may be disgusted with the experiment.

And yet, reflect! Have not all the best things in life come to you over your shoulder, and have not the great miseries of your life been due to not getting things you thought you ought to have, things you strived for?

Remember the simple and lively emotions caused by the unexpected stroke of luck, by the favor of some one from whom you did not look for it, by the love shown you that you did not dream of, by beautiful sights, pleasant odors, delightful foods, as well as other surprises of sympathy, regard, and appreciation that fell to you as bolts from a clear sky.

The best of our treasures came to us undeserved.

The joys that know no yesterdays are all surplus. We never earned them.

Health is nature's largess.

True love is the GIFT of an overbrimming heart. The man who thinks he DESERVES the love of a good woman, and the worship of little children, ought to be kicked.

In its higher plane, life is not commercial; it is not buying for a price; it is not a realm of law, except the mystic law of love. Thank God! we do NOT get our just deserts.

To get the taste of life we must approach it as a beggar at the king's court. If we are despised, what more natural? If we are feasted, what a marvel?

Rather, let us say that none of us can get the rich, sweet flavor of life unless he has the spirit in him of a little child.

Verily, verily, he that cannot be changed and become as a little child shall never know at all how good a thing it is to live.

THE SECRET OF PERMANENT PLEASURE

How can I get the most out of life?

How can I keep from having that sense of dissatisfaction from coming to bed with me of nights?

How can I have, for my visitor at the close of day, that feeling of content, that the gone twenty-four hours were worth while?

Tell me that. Tell me a cure for my disgust of self, for that ash-taste of self-consciousness, for that irritation in reflection, for that perpetual turning to to-morrow in order to drown the bitterness of to-day, as a fool turns to his cups to forget his life-weariness.

Well, this hint may help: THE SECRET OF PERMANENT PLEASURE LIES IN CULTIVATING EVER HIGHER FORMS OF PLEASURE.

The savage eats raw flesh, the civilized man wants it cooked, the more civilized man likes it well cooked.

The value of culture is the refinement of wants.

In a dumb, silly way the world perceives this, and tries to show superiority in forms of pleasure that are unusual, expensive, and exclusive. It dines at tawdry hotels, wears costly jewels, preens itself in fine clothes and wraps itself in rich furs.

This is the twisted, perverted notion of what is a great truth.

All luxury and extravagance soon become coarse and degrading to real souls. The Upper Ten get around to the crassness of life of the Submerged Tenth.

They are victims of the Great Delusion.

The Great Delusion is that it is Complexity that indicates higher life; whereas it is Simplicity, developing into ever greater Fineness (Refinement).

The roads to more permanent pleasures are these: Religion, Philosophy, Love, Art, Craftsmanship and Nature.

By Religion I mean a reverent habit of mind, a sense of wonder and mystery, a realization that we live in a world of spiritual meanings. Unless you can attain to this your life must always be mean and hard. Of course, I refer to no religious institution, but to that religious feeling that has always marked great lives.

By Philosophy I mean that you must have some sort of programme for your life. So long as events to you are but a disordered mess of "happenings" you will be miserable; the football of fate. You must have certain foundation principles, some settled theory of life that will bring order out of chaos.

By Love I mean that you must have the power to idealize your crude instincts. Lust sates, sickens, wearies. Love, which is the idealization of passion, is eternal, ever fresh.

By Art I mean the expression of the higher powers of the mind in creating beautiful things. When you learn to love a Greek Temple more than the gingerbread house of a New York millionaire, a painting by Israels or Millet more than a chromo, the wit of Charles Lamb more than that of Joe Miller, the charm of Michelangelo's "Moses" more than the huge parlor-clock monuments in some of our parks, a Beethoven quartet more than cabaret music, a story by Hawthorne more than one of the modern sex-soaked or adventure-choked romances, such a play as Barrie's "The Admirable Crichton" more than a cheap and loud melodrama, and, in general, all things that have the quietness of power, the self-restraint of genius and the subtlety of intellectual vision, then you have come considerably toward the point where your PLEASURES ARE MORE PERMANENT and have less nauseating dregs.

By Craftsmanship I mean that skill that transforms work from drudgery to enchantment.

And by the love of Nature I mean that patient study of, and eventual delight in, the marvellous design, perfection and handicraft exhibited by everything that grows, by everything the Creator has made.

THE SECRET OF PERMANENT PLEASURE will be found by any one who will make it his life business to seek his satisfaction in these six sources.

Thus you may come to that rational DELIGHT IN YOUR OWN THOUGHTS, such as Robert Bridges, the new laureate of England, expresses:

"My thoughts swim like a ship, that with the weight
Of her rich burden sleeps on the infinite seas
Becalm'd and cannot stir her golden freight."

SPANKING FATHER

THE country was agitated some days ago by the news of a gentleman from Indiana, a preacher, too, who had deemed it needful to spank his pa.

Although I have enrolled my name on the list of them who do not believe in spanking children, and have thereto set down many and cogent arguments, I do not wish to be taken as being opposed to spanking per se.

Spanking is a most wholesome and health-giving exercise, and is not without its mental and moral advantageous by-products.

Fathers often need it, and they are fortunate if they have sons husky enough to give them what they are suffering for.

Why, also, when innumerable children are being daily pounded a posteriori and nobody seems to think it's anybody's business to interfere, should all this hullabaloo arise when one child proceeds to turn the tables and castigate dad a bit? What are we coming to? Where is our personal liberty? Where the inviolability of family secrets? What next?

There are a lot of people who need spanking. Let me call a few to your mind.

There is the college youth putting in his nights and days in acquiring a set of ruinous habits and cultivating an assortment of snob notions, when he ought to be trying to learn something in return for the money his parents are advancing. He is going to be a gilded social bonehead, simply because there is no proper official to turn him over the knee and whale some sense into him.

There is the down-and-outer, the man who thinks the world is against him, who can't try again, and who believes there is nothing now left for him but to go out into the garden and eat worms. There's no use talking to him. The only remedy for his case is a tough hickory lath and a strong right arm.

There are the women who are so sorry for themselves, who have every disease they hear of, whose complaining whine is as the unceasing November rain upon the window. Of course we would not strike a woman; there ought to be a spanking machine.

Indeed, there is the whole army of self-pity; the weepers who rule their husbands by "the tyranny of tears"; the naggers, human mosquitoes, and "the female of the species is more deadly than the male"; the drunken loafers who "can't" quit making beasts of themselves; the gentlemen content to let their wives earn the living; the dudes and mashers who infest public ways, whose eyes insult every decent woman passing; the lackadaisical daughters who lounge about reading novels or manicuring their nails while mother washes the dishes; the egoist perky as a bantam rooster, and as pin-headed; and the whole dawdling set of idlers, who never dream of doing any of the world's work, are content to amuse themselves spending money other people have earned, and who, strange to say, look upon themselves as the superior class.

These to the shingle and the slipper! Let us have no "cruel and unusual" punishment, not the boot nor the wheel nor the Maiden of Nuremberg! No. Turn them gently up, and with the hairbrush or other handy instrument, and upon the place the Creator especially designed for correction unto the soul's health—soak 'em!

The question may arise, Who is going to decide which individuals are to be spanked? The answer is simple. If no one has any other nomination to offer, I will decide.

THINGS

Miss Mathilda Tommet of Milwaukee left a will the other day eight and one-half feet long, written in her own hand on sheets of paper pasted together. In it she bequeathed to one relative "my best bedspread and one-half of my best towels"; to another a high-backed chair, admonishing her executors to "be sure to take the one standing on the north side of the sideboard"; to another her chickens and feed; while vegetables, fruit, pickles, a pail of lard, and "father's old clock" go to another, and to her dearest enemy a pair of old shoestrings.

Then there was Thoreau, who in his house by Walden Pond would have no furniture; he found a stone once which he fancied, and kept awhile, but soon threw it away, as he found it had to be dusted.

One of the greatest tyrannies of life is Things.

The most common form of insanity is the mania to Own.

One of the first acts of a person who comes into money is to load himself down with a pile of rubbish that makes his life a fret and his deathbed terrible.

The very rich collect. They get together spoons, canes, pictures, vases, pitchers, books, or marbles. When there is no more room for them in the house they build a wing and pack it full.

I knew a man who had $20,000 worth of old postage stamps locked up in a safety deposit vault.

I knew an old woman who never travelled, although she longed to travel and had plenty of means, because she was afraid her parlor carpet and her blue china dishes would not properly be taken care of.

The stores are heaped up with THINGS. The most skilful men are employed to persuade people to buy THINGS for which they have no earthly use.

Every home contains sets of books that were bought at a high rate, and that have stood for years without a soul looking into them.

American living rooms are as cluttered as Westminster Abbey. Every mantel is loaded with junk. The walls are covered with pictures, most of them bad. The floors are so thick with chairs and superfluous stands and tables that few can wind their way through them by day and none by night.

Things, things, things! Bedrooms are full of them, closets heaped with them, the attic is choked with them, the woodshed and barn are running over.

When we go away on vacations we take trunks

full of things. When we go to Europe also we find that baggage is the plague of our life.

It is a relief to turn to the books of the Hindus and read:

"Even if they have longer remained with us, the objects of sense are sure to vanish. Why, then, not forsake them ourselves? If they pass away by themselves they cause the greatest pain to the mind, but if we forsake them ourselves they cause endless happiness and peace."

And in another Oriental book we find this searching word:

"For a man's life consisteth not in the abundance of THINGS which he possesseth."

THE HORROR OF JEWELS

YOU have read de Maupassant's story "The Diamond Necklace"? It tells of a poor and beautiful young wife who borrowed of a rich friend whom she had known in her school days a string of diamonds to wear to a ball. She lost the trinket. Her husband borrowed a great sum of money, had the necklace duplicated by a jeweller, and gave it to the rich woman, to avoid the charge of theft. The poor couple worked years to pay off the debt. The wretched woman, reduced to drudgery, lost all her beauty; became wrinkled, bent, old before her time. One day she met by chance her wealthy friend. They spoke of the necklace. The poor woman told the truth about her experience. The rich woman said it was too bad—for the necklace was but paste.

The tale is an artistic expression of what might be called The Horror of Jewels.

Almost every precious stone of great value, almost every $20,000 rope of pearls, or $1,000 solitaire diamond, or extraordinary ruby, has a history that runs to the accompaniment of vanity, envy, lust, theft, hate, and murder. Not one has produced any speck of real love or pure pcace of mind.

The Devil probably wears a million-dollar diamond ring. And his wife jewels running into the billions. They ought to.

The desire to own, wear, or collect gems of fabulous value is akin to the lowest cravings of which human beings are capable. It is an advertisement of offensive pride. It is provocative of unhappiness.

Precious gems are the seeds of those passions that destroy content.

To display them marks a certain lack of good breeding, of that gentleness that makes a gentleman.

They are the crystallized sap of the vicious inequity of privilege.

If one has money the worst form in which he can invest it is in the parade of gems.

The queer part of it is that you never can tell. Once we could distinguish real pearls from imitation by the person who wore them: if it was a lady with an income of fifty thousand a year they were genuine; if she was a working woman they were false. Nowadays the wealthy classes lock their real jewels in safety deposit vaults and wear imitation. They can arouse all the detestable emotions desired by wearing the false jewels, and run no risk of losing the real. The paste jewel holds the same "legal tender" relation socially to the true jewel that the ten-dollar bill holds commercially to the gold eagle.

Expensive jewels are of value to the rich as a

quick means of squandering their money and creating misery. "To us," says Gustave Tery, "there is no difference between a necklace costing a million francs and one costing three francs; but to the rich the difference is very real, since it comes, if I calculate correctly, to nine hundred and ninety-nine thousand nine hundred and ninety-seven francs. Which is not to be sneezed at."

IN PARIS

SHE was one of the most charming and well known artistes of the Théâtre Français. The other morning at an early hour she called a taxi to go to the railway station. She was to visit a sick friend in a near-by town. On arriving at the station she opened her handbag. Horrors! She found therein a handkerchief, some keys, a small mirror, and a powder box—but no money. She had forgotten her purse.

And the train was due to leave in ten minutes.

She got out of the taxi more frightened than she had ever been upon the stage, and addressed the chauffeur:

"Monsieur," she said, "something absurd has happened me, something desolating. I have left my pocketbook at home. I have no money to buy my railway ticket, no money to pay your fare."

The chauffeur smiled. The lady thereupon smiled also, an embarrassed smile, though she had a strong impulse to cry.

"If I dared, Monsieur," she said tremblingly, "I would ask you for a little money, instead of giving you some."

The chauffeur put his hand in his pocket.

"How much do you need, Madame?"

He had taken his purse from the pocket of his coat and was holding it politely in his hand.

The artiste, abashed, said:

"Oh, Monsieur, with fifty francs I——"

"Here you are, Madame!"

He handed her a fifty-franc note, which she took. At the same time she gave him her card, upon which she had written something.

"Here is my address," she said. "My husband will pay you. But—in the meanwhile—would you—may I offer you——"

She made a motion to remove her diamond ring. The chauffeur, with the manner of a gentleman, gave a gesture of protest.

"Oh! I pray you, Madame!" he said. "The card is quite enough."

She thanked him. She was furious, yet charmed. As she insisted in her very nicest words that he go get himself paid at once, he replied, with a shrug:

"Oh, yes, Madame, this evening, perhaps, or to-morrow, or next day. It doesn't matter in the least."

He smiled again, raised his cap, and, mounting his machine, disappeared.

No, this did not happen in New York, nor Chicago. I said Paris.

I think I read somewhere in Thackeray his account of a certain tailor in the Rue Something-or-other whom he owed a long-standing bill, and who, when Thackeray came to see him and apologized for not paying, not only expressed deep sympathy with his customer's embarrassment but even offered to lend him money. Such things do happen—in Paris.

FLAPDOODLE

"THE food on which fools are fed," says the Standard Dictionary.

In common use the term is the favorite one of cynics to characterize any sort of exuberance.

They also love the words "twaddle," "nonsense," "gush," and "balderdash."

The word cynic has the root-meaning of dog. It is a slander on the dog. The dog is the most sentimental animal known. He has a fit of ecstatic joy at even a glance from you.

When the lover makes a sonnet upon his mistress's eyebrow, it is Flapdoodle, to the cynic.

Read over your last letter, young lady, where he says your brow is like the snowdrift and your neck is like the swan, and your face it is the fairest that e'er the sun shone on. Flapdoodle!

Coo to your baby, little mother, and speak your infantile dialect, and ask him, "Does ums want to come to ums muzzers?" Flapdoodle!

Preach to the crowd gathered in the slums, O Salvation Army Lassie! Put tears in your voice, and make the spiritual appeal a red-hot heart force; bring the drunkard to sobriety and the smirched woman to repentance and a new life. Flapdoodle!

Plead for the cause of man, O social dreamer! Seek to put business upon a base of absolute justice, and to get for every human being equality of opportunity. Impractical! Flapdoodle!

Strive to abolish the accursed error of punishment, with its inhuman prisons and gallows trees, and substitute the organized prevention of crime and the scientific healing of the criminal. Flapdoodle!

Plead for the right of all children to play, to be duly equipped for life, and to be kept out of economic struggle by the mothering state. Flapdoodle!

Speak for the right of every woman to the full privilege of a human being. Flapdoodle!

Declare, O President of the United States, for the better way of self-restraint and patience, and against the medieval monstrosity of war, in dealing with a neighbor state. Flapdoodle!

Work, Mr. Lloyd George, for the protection of mothers, the alleviation of poverty, reforms in land holding, and the curbing of age-old privilege. All the Wise Ones cry out Flapdoodle!

Write, O Newspaper Man, not with dull prosing, but with the fire of conviction, words that throb like hearts alive. Flapdoodle!

So say the Critics, the Experienced, the Old-Hearted, the Sophisticated, the Burnt Out, from all whom the good God deliver us!

Give us, rather, the wonder of youth, the rapture of lovers, the gush of the enthusiastic, those that yet can weep over a book and wipe their eyes at a play, women who cuddle babies and are foolish over their husbands, men who can yell at a ball game and whoop at a political meeting, poets who still hear Pan's pipings, and patriots whose throats choke at the sight of their country's flag.

Thanks be! there are yet a thousand Fans, Sob Sisters, Giggling Girls, and Lovesick Swains to one Cynic! We wish him no harm, but one of him is a crowd.

STRANGE!

"WHAT fools these mortals be!" said Puck.

And we are inclined to agree with him when we observe:

That men toil their life long to lay up money for their children, when the worst calamity that can befall a youth is to be relieved from the need to work for a living;

That a man's pride and aim seems to be to keep his wife in idleness and luxury, and he considers himself disgraced if she engages in useful work, when the greatest foe to female virtue is idleness;

That all our greatness comes from struggle and danger, while we devote our lives to avoiding these things;

That the only faith that is worth anything is the product of wrestling with doubts, yet doubts we consider to be irreligious;

That all the world is convinced of the waste, stupidity, and madness of war, while each nation impoverishes itself still in the endeavor to prepare for war;

That individually we love our children better than anything in the world, while collectively, as a city, we leave no spaces for their playgrounds, but compel them to romp in the streets among the horses, street cars, and automobiles;

That we lock men up in prison as an antidote to crime, and when they come out they are more hardened criminals than before;

That we gather in churches and worship Jesus, yet consider as perfectly absurd and irrational the teachings He most insisted upon, deriding His faith in human nature, His law of love, and His principle of non-resistance; while the thing against which He warned us most strictly, the heaping up of money, is the one thing after which we are all mad;

That those of us most favored by fortune are in the heated pursuit of happiness, while we know very well that nobody who pursued happiness ever found it;

That we easily believe in selfishness and hate, which render us unhappy, while it is hard for us to believe in love and goodness, which make us happy;

That man should "put an enemy into his mouth to steal away his brains";

That politics is universally despised among us, while the only possible way to make a democracy successful is for every citizen to take an active interest in politics;

That the accepted method of preparing our sons and daughters for life is to send them to institutions sooted with medievalism, and while but one person in a hundred is by nature fitted to become a scholar or literary person, we continue the useless effort to make scholars out of those who are to become merchants, hand workers, salesmen, and housewives;

That while we all believe in majority rule, our cities are still governed by a compact minority composed of men of deficient character;

That we exert the greatest effort to be pleasant to strangers and mere acquaintances, for whom we care little or nothing, while we are neglectful, indifferent and often cruel to those we love most dearly;

That most of our worry is about the past, which is gone forever, and the future, which may never come, while we omit to enjoy to-day, which is all that we have to enjoy, and

That those who observe customs and conventions are called wise and safe, while those who believe in their reason, listen to the dictates of their heart, and trust their instinct are considered dangerous, if not wicked.

WHAT'S THE MATTER WITH ART?

SHORTLY after the first production of the opera "Nail," at Paris, I met its composer, Mr. Isadore Lara, who, I found, saw eye to eye with me on the question, "What's the Matter With Art?"

"The trouble is," he said, in substance, "that opera is controlled by a small class of people. It ought to belong to the whole people."

In other words, that same thing is the matter with art that is the matter with almost everything else, to wit: class.

Like every other department of human activity, art awaits the liberating touch of democracy.

Like everything else, art can have nothing so bad happen to it as to be patronized.

So long as the artist is dependent upon the caprice of millionaires and kings, it will be hampered.

The best friend of the artist is the people. What he needs is a public, not a patron.

To serve the public gives a man freedom, mastery, inspiration. To please a patron invariably produces the spirit of a valet.

First of all, the public must be brought to realize that art is not the plaything of the rich, but the food of the whole community. That it is civilizing, refining, has distinct human value.

When it reaches this point it will pay its artists. It will provide scope, in its public halls, churches, galleries, and parks, for the painter and sculptor.

It will maintain, each city its own opera house, where the masterpieces of all ages can be given at prices the people can afford to pay.

It will abolish the "star" nuisance.

The singers and players will be chosen from among each country's own youth. We shall go to hear, not Caruso or Tetrazzini, but La Tosca and the Mastersingers.

So far from democracy meaning the universal dulness of mediocrity, it means opportunity for real superiority; it means merit to the front, and the contempt of push, pull, influence, and money.

As monarchy has been abolished in America in the realm of politics, as hierarchy has been put by in religion, and as we are working to get wealth into the control of the whole people, instead of a few, so art needs to be delivered from patronage and made a public good.

THE AMERICAN PENAL SYSTEM

It is hard, it is almost impossible, for advocates of a change in custom or government to get out from under a charge which has worn down to a platitude.

The average man refuses to think, when he can get his thinking ready-made.

For instance, we, who believe that prisons and punishments are wrong, are generally classed with the sentimental perverts who pet criminals, with the women who carry bouquets to murderers, weep over the sad lot of burglars that have been justly laid by the heels, and want to feed them pie.

Allow us, therefore, to clearly state our point of view.

We are not opposed to the present prison system because of pity for jail birds. We are sorry for them, as any human being is sorry to witness suffering, but if their punishment were good for them or for society at large we would gladly applaud their stripes.

But our position is this: that THE FACTS IN THE CASE PROVE beyond any reasonable doubt that the theory of punishment is both impotent for good and fruitful of evil.

Why do we punish a thief or robber, for example? For three reasons only.

First, to protect the community against him. We incarcerate him, shave his head, put him at hard labor, isolate him, or even hang him, so that innocent citizens may be safe from his pernicious activities.

Second, we punish him to "teach him a lesson," to change him and make him an honest man.

Third, it is also to give an example to other evildoers and by fear to dissuade them from crime.

All very well. The only trouble is, that sending a man to the penitentiary does NOT result in any of these benefits.

As a rule, which any intelligent prison keeper will verify, the convict who has served his time comes back to society A WORSE CRIMINAL THAN WHEN HE WENT TO PRISON. From being an ordinary man, who committed a crime by impulse, he has become a member of the hardened criminal class and is a greater menace to the commonwealth than ever.

As a rule, instead of prison changing him to an honest man, it MAKES HIM A MORE VICIOUS MAN. It destroys the little good character he had.

And, as a rule, instead of his punishment deterring others it psychologically DEVELOPS MORE CRIMINALS.

Why, therefore, keep up a system that is

proved by experience and reason to work precisely contrary to what we expected it to work?

It is a pleasure to note that the more intelligent of the lawyers themselves are with us. At least they cannot be accused of maudlin sentimentality. At a recent meeting of the American Bar Association, at Montreal, at which session William H. Taft was chosen president, Mr. Moorfield Storey of Massachusetts declared the American penal system a failure.

"Our prisons are manufactories of criminals, and it is time we changed our whole method of dealing with convicts," he said.

"All convicted persons should be turned over to a commission charged with full responsibility for their care and custody under an indeterminate sentence, with authority to release them at such time and on such terms as would guarantee their future harmlessness to society.

"IN OTHER WORDS, WE SHOULD TREAT CRIMINALS RATHER AS SICK MEN THAN AS BAD MEN, AND OUR PLACES OF CONFINEMENT AS HOSPITALS RATHER THAN AS PRISONS."

IN PRAISE OF LAZINESS

I MAKE no bones of it, but here confess and set down that I am lazy. I was born lazy and it has grown on me. I would never move at all if it did not hurt so to remain in one position. The only reason I take exercise is in order to relax afterward.

Furthermore, I raise my voice in defense of the army of the lazy ones. They are the salt of the earth.

A lazy person does better work than an industrious body. He puts a fiery energy into his task because he wants to finish it as soon as possible.

A lazy boy will saw wood fast so that he can get through and rest. A lazy girl sweeps the room with whirlwind activity, while the girl who loves work will fiddle about all morning.

It is laziness that is the spring of human progress.

Because a lazy man wanted to get out of the job of currying the horse, he thought out a plan for putting a bucket of gasoline under the buggy seat, whereby we ride like the wind.

Because lazy folks hated to climb stairs, elevators were invented.

Because people were too lazy to get off the train and go to the lunch counter, they devised dining cars; and being too lazy to ride on the railway all night sitting up, they contrived sleeping cars.

Being too lazy to dip his pen in the ink every few seconds, some genius invented the fountain pen. And being too lazy even to use that, he proceeded to build a typewriter. Also too lazy to run the typewriter himself, he started the fashion of having girl typists.

It was a lazy genius that thought of making a patent cigar lighter out of a flint stone and benzine, because he was too tired to strike matches.

Likewise, who would have conceived the idea of a fireless cooker except some woman too lazy to stand over the cook stove?

The eight-day clock is due to the unwillingness of men to wind the thing up every evening; and now they have clocks that will run a year.

The coat-shirt is the triumph of laziness too great to put the garment on over one's head, in the good old style.

It is to almighty laziness we owe the ocean liner, the electric telegraph, the baby wagon, the buggy spring, Cook's tours, the shoe-horn and the works of Mark Twain.

It is told of the last named that when he worked in a newspaper office he would pay the office boy a nickel to sweep around him so that he would not have to take his feet off the table.

If everybody was an earnest and toiling little Willie that just ate up work and loved to employ every moment in useful energy, we should lapse into barbarism.

It is because the race is so blamed trifling and shiftless that it forges ahead.

THE LADIES' CARD GAME

I NEVER understood the calling business until one day I found my small children, with the children of some of the neighbors, playing in the nursery. They had a number of cards and were depositing them, with much ceremony, at various chairs about the room.

Then I saw. It is a GAME.

Compared to calling, football and baseball are second rate in popularity.

It is a game especially for ladies, more especially for those fair ones who are hobbled by no useful occupation. It is played as follows:

You take a deck of cards, more properly speaking, a package of cards; nice, new, white cards, which the lady in charge of the stationery at the department store will have printed for you, according to Hoyle.

Then you foot it, or if you live in a city where distances are great, you hire a cab; or if you want to appear the indubitable thing you own a vehicle with your monogram on the door, and you go to all the houses on your list.

Arriving at the door you ring the bell. A servant appears. You ask if Mrs. Van Dunsensnipper is at home.

If she is, you go into the parlor and wait till she gets her hair fixed. When she comes down you engage in a little short and pleasant conversation; the shorter the pleasanter.

If she is not at home you leave a certain number of your cards with the maid, which is still pleasanter. I don't know what the right number is, but it is very important.

You check the lady off your list. By and by all the ladies you have dealt cards to come around to your house and deal.

That this is a game is proved by the fact that it is fatal, unforgivable, to make a mistake. In business, when you make an error, you apologize and pay up and go ahead. But in a game, when you make a slip, you're OUT.

A male friend of mine observed that he couldn't guess what the Sam Hill it was all about. But he was plain ignorant. There are also people that do not enjoy baseball.

If the ladies want to play cards in a taxicab, let them alone. It is more healthful, to say the least, than playing poker in the Black Hole of Calcutta, otherwise known as the card room of the club.

LOVE AND WISDOM

A CORRESPONDENT writes: "When people are married we often hear, 'What could he or she see in the other?'

"Does love give a deeper insight and see a worth really there, or does it merely overheat the fancy to imagine a worth not there?

"Will you give an explanation of this?"

I will. Because there are few questions of deeper concern to thousands than this.

For practical purposes, for living one's life in peace and happiness, it is more important to know about the laws of love than the laws of chemistry or of the United States.

The question asked by my correspondent is a great big vital one, up to date, and almost a matter of life and death.

Here, therefore, is the answer: *Love is not a delusion. Love is the only thing that can see truth.*

That is true not only in the relation of men and women but everywhere else.

The reason Edison is a wizard at invention is not only because of his genius, but also because he loves his laboratory work.

No man can handle a horse who does not love a horse.

The best cook is the best lover of cooking.

The greatest baseball player is the most tremendous lover of the game, other things being equal.

The best novelist or story writer is the one who most wholly loves the characters he creates.

The best actor is the greatest lover of his art.

The only preacher of any account is the one who is infatuated with preaching.

There is only one potency. It is love. There is only one vision. It is love. There is only one wisdom. It is love. There is only one religion. It is love.

You cannot get anything out of a book unless you love it.

You cannot teach children unless you love them.

Money never did any permanent good in the world. One loving heart outweighs all the gifts of Carnegie and Rockefeller in its results on the welfare of mankind.

Love sees. It is not blind. Indifference is blind. The cold heart is blind.

There is only one tragedy. It is when love dies.

Love creates. Coldness is impotent.

Love has that faith (trust) which saves the world. Intellect has those doubts which unloose the world. Love is synthetic. Intellect is analytic.

The bottommost pit of hell, Dante says, is frozen; the seat of the Eternal in heaven glows with heat and light.

The Devil, Mephistopheles, according to Goethe, is pure intellect. "He never loved a human soul."

"God," says the Bible, "is love."

This earth was made for lovers, and he who loves not, though he be walking about, is dead, dead, dead.

THE SICK ROOM

THE newspaper pages are filled with tides of vigorous life. Advertisers exploit their goods, theatres display their attractions, there are the activities of crime, of politics, of sport; the virile stream of humanity leaps and sparkles beneath the reader's eye.

And all the while a great part of these readers are in a condition where the arena of strife does not interest them, and the warmth of the world's blood chills them. I speak of the sick.

They are shut up in darkened bedrooms, they lie in hospital wards, they sit solitary by the window of the sitting-room, or hobble about with crutch or cane. They are the wounded in life's battle, the driftwood upon the banks of life's stream.

So here's a word for them.

Do not imagine that because you are not well you are out of the game. Opportunity is still yours. Some of the best and finest work done for the human race is done by the sick people.

You may no longer be a centre of active work in the business of money-getting, you cannot go to your office nor attend to your house, but you can do better than that. You can be a centre of cheer and encouragement to all who know you.

If you will put away self-pity, if you will not complain, if you will be just as courageous and intelligent in the business of being unwell as you were in the street and mart when you were well, if in your weakened body you will maintain a stout heart, you cannot realize how you will radiate life and power into all who come in contact with you.

The sick room may be the temple of the house.

There's a little old blind grandmother in a certain home who, by her spirit of sanity and her sense of human values, has reconciled her daughter and son-in-law who were drifting toward alienation, brought a wayward granddaughter and a foolish college grandson to their senses, and governs that household not with a rod of iron but with a fairy wand of subtler power.

There is a man, once active in great affairs, a figure in the money world, but now sitting helpless with paralysis. He is just as brave and hopeful now as ever. Around his affliction have bloomed priceless flowers of love and tenderness, of whose existence he was never before aware.

Your sickness may be a privilege. It will show you, if you can take it heroically, the very best things in life.

You are out of the game of getting-on, but you are placed where certain factors of life of inestimable value may be made clear and usable to you.

In fact, the best part of living is not monopolized by the healthy people. Sickness has its spirit-compensations. Life is very great and wide and high, it has vast mysteries that active people miss. It has reaches of thought and feeling they cannot know.

In your quiet room you may find your soul, your real self; you may have experiences so rich and strange that, when you grow well again, if so be that shall come to pass, you will look back upon these shaded and idle days, as the traveller who has crossed the desert remembers the oasis.

UP AGAINST IT

It is a terse Americanism, and expresses in solid, idiomatic language a solid, bitter fact: "Up Against It."

There's an army of them right in this city, an army of soldiers that battle for sustenance, an army fighting in the last ditch.

I saw and talked with one the other day. She was a mere child, just twenty-two. Her clothes were not new. Her neck was thin, her cheeks thin, her eyes, it seemed, too large.

"I am still trying to get a job," she said. "Oh! I'm pretty well; only I haven't as much strength as I had. You see, when I don't eat regularly it tells on me. I don't eat every day, and some days I only get one meal. And then I walk from where I room to the business places downtown. It's a long way. I get awful tired. My landlady is awful good to me. She's waiting till I get my job. Gee! it's fierce to be up against it!"

Yet withal she was brave, cheerful, self-respecting, keeping her soul and her little body clean, while she fought with the wild wolves that hunt in cities.

"I got a raise yesterday," said a young man,

a friend of mine. "I pawned my watch. I had a grand feed."

He had come to the city to study music. Oh! the heart-breaking company of them that hope to live by music! For every singer in a church choir, getting $5 a Sunday, twenty stand hungry for the place. For every girl in the theatre chorus, twenty have been turned away to tramp further. For every clerk in the stores there are three in line waiting, up against it.

It is the firing line of civilization.

It is the thin red line we have thrown out to meet the common enemy, Hunger.

Late at night I have seen them on the benches in the parks, sitting with a newspaper over the knees. There seems to be a deal of warmth in a newspaper. I have talked with them. They are sociable folks, much easier to approach than successful people.

I have always loved failures. They are more human. Their souls seem more visible than the souls of the prosperous.

Where the Salvation Army's drums are beating and horns blowing they congregate. That is my favorite church. Surely if the Messiah is anywhere He may be found there.

You can see them in the saloons. A glass of beer can be got for five cents. It is the little bit of light in lives most terribly dark.

They are not all tramps. There are mothers up against it, holding babies, looking all night into the darkness, as if into the eyes of Pauguk.

There are hard-working fathers who have plodded all day searching for what means more to them than salvation—a job.

There are boys, for whom crime bids.

There are girls, for whom human tigers lie in wait.

There are little children. I saw two, a little boy and girl, the other morning early; they were going through a garbage can, looking for scraps of food.

Those who have never been up against it do not know what a tragic world this is.

THE KITCHEN

IF I ever get money enough to build a house of my own the first thing I shall construct will be the kitchen.

The kitchen is to the home what the stomach is to the body. The Greeks used to think the soul was located in the stomach, and it wasn't a bad guess. Certain it is that you cannot see much glory in the universe while you have any kind of a stomachache.

My kitchen will be five things: big, light, clean, well equipped, and comfortable to loaf in.

To begin with the last, I do not see why a man who owns a house should be excluded from an essential part of it. Why should I be condemned to sit always in the front room surrounded by uncomfortable furniture, slippery floors, and fragile bric-a-brac, while the hired girl enjoys a neat, homey kitchen?

When I feel like it I want to occupy a cane rocker by the window, look around upon shining brass stewpans, and read in the recipe book how to make ginger cookies.

And then the sounds of the kitchen. They are more intimately lovely than any other house-voices. First and foremost the song of the tea kettle: it just sings home and mother and solid comfort right into the core of your everlasting soul. Then the roar of the fire in the stove, the bubbling of the pot where the potatoes are boiling, the angry sputter of ham frying, and above all the solemn tick-tock of the old clock, beating time like an orchestra leader over the whole performance.

Also come the odors of the kitchen; the fragrance of bread just out of the oven, of the fowl done to a turn, filling the air with an aroma beyond that of flowers, and, Lord bless us all! if that isn't a real pumpkin pie the cook has just delivered into the world! It is an event that should be celebrated with cheer and song.

The eye feasts likewise. I want a floor of old-fashioned red brick on my kitchen floor; in all the realm of art no color is so rich. I want the copper utensils to gleam like burnished shields upon the shelf. I want to see the flash of the Sabatier knives in a row on the wall, weapons in the noble war of gastronomy. I want to see the old Delft-blue bowls and brown cooking vessels round about. Besides, there are the whiteness of white flour on the biscuit board, the sparkling heaps of sugar, the rosy-cheekedness of apples, the orangeness of oranges, and the grapeness of grapes.

There is no place where you can feel so human as in the kitchen. When you are tired of being respectable, and your soul is sick of good clothes, oh, to come aside a while here, in slippers and shirt-sleeves, and in the cane rocker aforesaid read in peace in your daily paper all the antics of this mountebank world!

And then—best of all—the little boy comes in, you know what he wants, and although it is against the rules, you steal for him two Jonathan apples and three sugar cookies; he beams undying love at you, and skips out before mother sees him, while you, partner in such delicious crime, read your paper as if nothing had happened.

SUPERFLUOUS ENERGY

ONE of the most astounding things in nature is the waste of sun-force. Frank W. Very, in an article in the *Popular Science Monthly,* calls attention to this, saying:

"The earth is a mere point in space, and receives no more than one 2,200,000,000th of the radiant energy the sun is outpouring so lavishly." Yet from this almost infinitesimal fraction of the sun's total radiation practically all known forces on earth are due.

The power of wind and wave and tide, of fire and its son, steam, of plant and animal life, of glacial movement, of rain and snow, even of all growth in trees and herbs and all forms of animal energy, come from this crumb of solar potency caught by the whirling world.

And this apparent waste and extravagance characterizes all nature, and men and their spiritual dynamics.

It is a law of mind. You cannot learn one fact alone. Your study, your experience, must embrace a myriad of facts; only so will the one remain with you.

From months and years of "practice" the pianist culls at last the flower of perfection.

You read a book of 400 pages, and are lucky if one paragraph sticks.

To make forty sales the department store must induce 400 customers to come and look.

The travelling salesman interviews twenty merchants to get three or four who will place orders with him.

This is the law of success: Keep trying; if you want one man to give you employment or buy your wares you must apply to many men.

Out from every soul pours the power of personal influence. All but a minute fraction of it seems wasted, as in the case of the sun. You must be kind a thousand times to be effectually kind once. You must forgive seventy times seven to find the one instance where forgiveness counts. A hundred times must you be courageous if you hope to be brave the one time when it will be worth while.

The teacher knows how in the schoolroom she must sow beside all waters to make a few seeds grow.

An editor writes one appeal in his daily newspaper. A hundred thousand copies are bought. Perhaps 5,000 persons glance at his article. Five hundred read it through. One hundred are interested. Ten perhaps are persuaded.

Of the countless volumes of philosophy, how rare are those that reach and fecundate the receptive mind!

What becomes of all the wasted energy of

suns, souls, books and all powers, physical and spiritual? We do not know. We believe that somehow Nature, in her nicely balanced adjustments, throws nothing away, and transforms into other kinds of energy all superfluous vigor.

But the observer may learn, if he be wise, not to be discouraged at the apparent fruitlessness of his effort, but to go on, as the sun for many millions of years has gone on, putting forth his full vitality, that some fragment be used.

WHY WAS I BORN?

THERE is one question upon the answer to which rests the success or failure of life.

It is the question: "Why was I born?"

A strange fact is that nobody knows the answer. The purpose which the Creator had in mind when He made me has never been known, never will be known.

Curious that the most fateful of all problems should be forever unanswerable!

We may BELIEVE this or that to be the reason why we were created; we cannot KNOW.

Notwithstanding this fact, the net result of my life depends upon THE THEORY I form to answer this query.

But how can I tell which theory is best when there is no means of knowing which is true?

There is a way to tell which theory is, if not true, at least approximately true. This way is suggested by what is called PRAGMATISM.

That is to say: That answer to the question is most likely to be true WHICH WILL WORK.

We cannot answer the question "Why was I born?" by investigating CAUSES. The secrets of life are beyond us. The Creator will not be interviewed.

But we can select an answer by noting RESULTS. For instance:

"I was made in order that I might get all the pleasure possible out of life." This solution means wreckage. Its fallacy is proved by insane hospitals, feeble-minded asylums, and by those murders, adulteries, and heart-breaks that constantly attend the end of the pleasure seeker.

"I was made in order that I might escape this evil world and get safely into a better one after death." Such an answer leads logically to the asceticism that marked the dark ages and the hard morbidity that characterized Puritanism.

"I was born to labor for others" means a race of slaves.

"I was born to live and to enjoy myself upon the fruits of others' labor" means a class of snobs.

The most satisfactory answer, in twentieth century terms, is: "I was born to express what forces my Creator planted in me; to develop my instincts and talents under the guidance of reason; to find permanent happiness by fostering the higher, more altruistic, and spirit impulses and by subduing the violence of the more brutal impulses. I was born to find love and my own work, and through these liberty. In one word the purpose of creating me was that I should be as GREAT as possible."

Only by this answer do we get strength without cruelty, virtue without narrowness, beauty without effeminacy, love without contamination, reverence without superstition, joy without excess.

I do not KNOW this answer is correct. I BELIEVE it to be the MOST NEARLY correct for the simple reason that IT WORKS.

THE OUTPOPULATING POWER

THERE is a war constantly going on. It is not of axe upon helm, shot upon armor plate, duels of death-spitting dreadnoughts, nor airplanes dropping bombs upon a sleeping city.

It is a deeper battle, subterranean as instinct, unseen as nature's hidden laws.

Deep as the cause of the running of sap in spring. Deep as the reason why Sahara is parched and the Mississippi Valley is watered.

A battle unnoticed as glacier movements, irresistible as the succession of geologic eras, pitiless as Time, sure as the precession of the equinoxes.

It is the battle of blood against blood, race against race, stock against stock.

It is the war of the powers of procreation.

It is the elemental competition in fecundity.

"What constitutes a state?" asks Sir William Jones; and answers his question: "Not cities proud with spires and turrets crowned; not bays and broad armed ports, where laughing at the storm rich navies ride; but—men"; and his conclusion should be mended; let us rather say, "women."

The state's ultimate armament is the strong, breeding woman.

Not the war cries of bearded hosts but the lusty cries of the army of babies are the terrible menace of destiny.

Sex perversion means the end of the world, the people extinguished in madness. Sex uncleanness means a race rushing toward its Day of Judgment.

England builds battleships; it were far better she gave heed to the fact that her population is decreasing.

The profoundest crime of American plutocracy is that it will not breed, and spreads the death-gospel of childlessness to others.

Look at the fashion papers, the newest models in gowns, latest hints from Paris; and see the tendency of upper-tendom toward the ideal of Kipling's "damn thin-hipted woman"; man's plaything, not his creative mate!

Observe the universal fear of the responsibilities of marriage, the dread of children, the expressed creed of a weak race that one should not have children until one has gained a competence! The pioneers who hewed the path for the Golden West had no such puling timidity.

In the long evolutionary strife for the survival of the fittest that nation shall conquer that shall not shrink from applying science to the procreation of itself; that shall study eugenics as the key-problem of destiny; that shall drive out sex-perversion from life and literature with the whip of life-preserving scorn; that shall idealize with the utmost beauty of poet and romancer the mating of its young; that shall tear the veils of false modesty and criminal ignorance from the sex instinct and replace them with the halo of truth, knowledge, and self-reverence; that shall reject the mediæval shame of nature and take pride in its virility; that shall exalt in its heart and support and protect with all its resources the woman who bears children and devotes her life to their bringing up.

For the vanguard of a nation's conquest, and the last citadel of its defense, is not the armed man nor the war machine; it is THE MOTHER.

INTELLIGENT OPTIMISM

There is an intelligent optimism, and there are several varieties of fool optimism.

There is a theological optimism that claims to have proved that this is "the best possible world"; it is a hopefulness built on logic, and is rather unconvincing to the modern mind.

There is a kind of self-willed optimism, an assumption that all is well whether it's well or not, a postulating, assertive optimism that grins even at funerals, from a sense of duty. People of this cult are rather trying. They are always telling you that "all is for the best" when you know very well that certain things are for the worst.

Intelligent optimism, however, does not declare that all is good, including the devil and disease, but it asserts that the general law of progress is upward, that there is much good in things as they are, that it is conducive to our comfort and efficiency to let our minds dwell upon that rather than upon the evil, and that we are capable of making things better and propose to do so.

Our confidence in the constant improvement of the world is not a matter of faith. We do not need to shut our eyes, cross our fingers, and repeat a creed. Our assurance is based upon knowledge. An understanding of history, of the conditions of society in former times compared to this time, and of the steady growth of liberty and civil rights, forms the foundation of our conclusion.

Further ground for our hopefulness consists in our realization that it is in men's power to improve the world they live in. We are finding out that human welfare grows, not only by Providence or superhuman "laws," but also by our own efforts. By organized exertion we have overturned tyrannies, abolished slavery, removed plagues, and rendered life in the twentieth century a hundred times more agreeable than it was in the eighteenth. What we have done we can continue to do. We can go on improving our state, we can produce wealth less wastefully and distribute profits more fairly, we can raise the condition of the workingman, liberate woman, give children better training, curb swollen fortunes and wealth-combinations, take better care of our unfortunates, and do much toward preventing crime and poverty. We no longer look to kings and nobles to do those things for us, we no longer merely pray and hope for the Deity to do them, we are conscious of the ability to help along by our own activities. Hence our optimism.

But optimism is not only a logical affair. It is a state of mind, a temperamental product. Wherever you find health, vigor, and work, you find optimism. Pessimism is a secretion of a morbid mind, of weakness, anemia or idleness.

We are optimists because we are better fed, housed, and clothed, have more books and newspapers, have the remedy for social wrongs in our own hands in the agency of democracy, and in short have a faith and joy in life and its possibilities not based upon tradition or authority, but upon facts, upon instincts, and upon the consciousness of our own strength.

That is why this great people front the future with "morning faces," and refuse to melt in fear at the alarms of the calamity-howlers.

THE SCRAP PILE

THE human scrap pile.

The refuse, the discard, the useless, the non-producers, the wasters, the parasites, the loafers, the do-nothings, the consumers of unearned food, the wearers of given clothes, the stalled, fattened, curried, sleek human animals devouring the substance of them that sweat and toil.

Wherever you find an idle group you find a septic point in mankind.

Among the "rights of man" there is no right to work not.

The conscience of the Twentieth Century thunders the commandment of Carlyle: "Find thy work! Produce! Produce! In God's name, produce!"

The prosperity of America is attacked already by that species of vermin that always infest accumulated wealth, vested privilege, old-standing institutions.

The tramps, hoboes, and slum loafers are not our severest menace. The unemployed rich men, who do nothing but amuse themselves and spend their own or their father's money, are just as bad.

The women who flit from northern fashionable resort hotels in summer to southern fashionable hotels in winter, who spend their days in motoring and their evenings at cards, whose whole energy is occupied in dress and schemes of precedence, are but particles of that heap of waste and poison that must be swept away before democracy shall find a basis of justice and peace. They are the seed of the coming revolution. They are the kindlings for the cleansing fires of Destiny.

There is direct connection between the workhouse convicts and the hangers-about at the snob palaces of American plutocracy.

A. A. McCormick, president of the County Board of Cook County (Chicago), speaking of the efforts being made to put paupers and outcasts to work, observed:

"The human scrap pile for which we have to pay is cluttered up, not alone with the paupers and the 'down and outs,' but with the idle rich, who sit around luxurious hotels and watering places with nothing to do but overeat and sleep. I was astounded by the waste of human energy at the county institutions, but I am appalled when I think of that far greater waste of energy among those whose wants have been provided for and who have nothing to do but dress for dinner.

"We have 2,500 persons sitting with folded hands in our county institutions, content because their wants have been provided for. I could not help thinking of our wealthy outcasts in this connection. They are really beyond the pale of human effort, for they are doing nothing that is of good to anybody, not even to themselves.

"The idle wealthy are going on the scrap pile voluntarily. They are not only useless but harmful. Somebody ought to wake them up and make them think."

AISCHROLATREIA

AISCHROLATREIA is a word used by Frederic Harrison, and his definition of it is "the worship of the ugly, the nasty, and the brutal."

The human soul has its laws as fixed as the laws of the human body. Feed the body enough alcohol and you will get delirium tremens. Feed the soul enough sensual emotion, and cultivate it with introspection, and you get aischrolatreia.

Any egotism is bad, but emotional egotism is poison.

The best part of life is feeling, but it is always the best things that are most liable to excess. Beyond a certain point enthusiasm becomes madness, love becomes perversion, and the taste for beauty becomes the taste for the hideous.

Even in religious emotion this is true. As Charles H. Spurgeon said, "Excessive spirituality is akin to sensuality."

The antidote to toxic emotion is work, accomplishment, activity. Where one has no task, no pressure of duty, the soul rots. It is the idle class that is the dangerous class, because having no work the soul gives itself over to the search for new sensations. This is as bad as taking opium, cocaine, or whiskey.

The first buds of passion in the soul are the most exquisitely beautiful of all human experience. Give yourself over to the pursuit of passion, however, and your end will be the most horrible torture conceivable.

Cubism and Futurism in art are the results of unrestrained love of beauty; they are that hideousness into which egoistic emotional drunkenness leads. After a while the art drunkard finds no satisfaction in the simplicities of nature; nothing but the distorted can arouse him, just as after a while the victim of alcoholism has no taste for beer or honest wine, but must have absinthe, mescal, or vodka.

It was because of the cumulative danger of pleasure, when followed solely, that the Puritans sought to prohibit it. But the master word of morality is not prohibition; it is self-control. Life needs love, beauty, laughter, and its measure of rational inebriation. Without these the soul hardens. Yet with these, and without self-control, the soul fevers and decays.

The law of life is not "Never!" It is "Never too much!" This was the motto of Socrates.

A good example of the ruin of over-emotionalism is found in the poet Baudelaire. He gave himself up to feeling and to analyzing the emotions of his inner life. Typical of his philosophy are these words from one of his prose-poems:

"One must ever be drunken. Everything is in that; it is the only question. In order not to feel the horrible burden of Time that is breaking your shoulders, bending you earthwards, you must be ceaselessly drunken.

"But with what? With wine, poetry, or virtue, as you will—only intoxicate yourself; and if sometimes, on the steps of a palace, on the greensward of a grave, or in the mournful solitude of your room, you wake to find the intoxication diminished or vanished, ask of the wind, or the wave, or the star, or the bird, or the clock . . . ask what time it is; and the wind, wave, star, bird, and clock will tell you: 'It is time to be drunken.' Lest you should be the martyred slaves of Time, be ceaselessly drunken! With wine, poetry, or virtue, as you will."

The life of Baudelaire went out in the impotence of despair, the agony of self-torture. His beauty worship finished in aischrolatreia. His sterile genius left nothing to mankind.

Compare his sentiment with that of another man who gave as his life-motive: "I must work the works of him that sent me, while it is day; for the night cometh when no man can work." The life of this man has been a fountain of inexhausted passion for a thousand years.

THE MIRTH CURE

THERE are all manner of cures, from mud baths and Perkins's Patent Porous Plaster up to Thought Vibrations, but the grandest of all is the Mirth Cure.

It keeps well in any climate, is guaranteed under the pure food and drug law, doesn't cost a cent, and has helped others. Why not you?

The formula is found in the writings of the wisest man, who was a Jewish king and philosopher. He said:

"A merry heart doeth good like a medicine."

Note—he did not say a merry wife, though she certainly does good. (Perhaps he had too many wives and was afraid he would be asked which one.)

He did not say a merry husband, though he helps some.

Nor did he say merry children, nor a merry house, nor a merry occupation, nor any such thing.

For his wise old eyes saw too deeply into life to make the mistake of supposing that circumstances are the root of joy. He knew that the real fountain of mirth is the heart.

If you have a merry heart it makes no difference what may be your position, whether you be a tramp on the road, a scrubwoman in an office building, a brakeman, a street car conductor, a merchant man, or even a college president. You are an electric light in the fog of human despondency, sunshine breaking through earth-sorrow clouds, water to parched souls.

Did you ever hear the story of "The Happy Man's Shirt?" It is an old one, but one of those that ought constantly be retold.

There was once a king who was smitten with sadness and disgust of life. He had gorged at all human pleasures, could no more be amused, and now was like to die.

They called in the soothsayers and medicine men, but none could suggest a remedy. At last they sent to an old hermit who lived in the wood, who said: "The case is simple. Let the king sleep all night in a happy man's shirt, and he will be healed."

Whereupon the king ordered that the palace be searched, a happy man be found and his shirt brought. But no happy man could be discovered in the palace.

Then they sought through the city and then throughout the length and breadth of the kingdom, but no man could they lay hands upon who would declare, without reservation or secret evasion of mind whatever, that he was entirely happy.

A little group of the king's courtiers were returning home disconsolate, and as they rode along the highway they espied a beggar sitting under a tree, playing with the autumn leaves and smiling to himself.

"Hola!" they shouted. "Are you happy?"

"Surely!" replied the beggarman.

"Why, you're nothing but a beggar! You don't know where you are going to get your dinner, do you?"

"Oh, no. But it isn't dinner time yet. I had a good breakfast."

Then they told him of the king's plight and besought him to give them his shirt forthwith, adding that it should be returned to him filled with gold pieces.

At that the ragged man lay back on the grass and laughed as if he would expire.

"Come," said the royal attendants, "we have no time for trifling. Off with your shirt, or we will jerk it off."

"Hold hard, gentlemen," said the beggar, striving to control his mirth. "That is just what I am laughing at. I AIN'T GOT NO SHIRT!"

So they went and told the king that but one happy man could be unearthed in all his realm, and that one was shirtless.

And the king had sense enough to perceive that happiness does not depend on the shirt you sleep in, nor the bed on which you lie, nor the house that covers you—no, nor any external thing, but comes from the heart within you.

Thus was he cured, and arose and went about his business; and thus also may you be cured, if so be that there is still left unparalyzed in you the power to THINK.

DISCARDED THINGS

THE secret of health is the elimination of waste.

The first thing the physician prescribes usually is a physic. No matter what ails the patient it hardly ever can be a mistake to see that the body is well rid of its waste. If the organs of excretion go on a strike it is fatal.

The same law holds in affairs. Every business man knows what pains he must take to keep his desk clean, and how papers will accumulate on the table and get choked into pigeonholes and obstipate letter files and pile up in drawers and cases. There are so many things we are not quite ready to do to-day, and to-morrow finds us still indecisive, and so the documents drift into forgotten holes and before long the desk is a jungle of undone matters.

It takes moral courage to use the waste basket vigorously.

Some men can work in litter, with papers on their desk like snowdrifts, papers stuffed bulging full into boxes, papers on the floor about them "thick as autumnal leaves that strew the vale of Vallombrosa," but I don't understand how they do it. An unanswered letter haunts me like the ghost of Banquo. An unpigeonholed receipt on my table irritates me like a fly.

The art of life is to discard.

Progress is clogged by the persistent remnants of the outworn past.

Clogged! clogged! clogged! That is the story of the Church, the School, the State.

Clogged with moth-eaten ideas, with traditional passions, with antiquated ideals, with petty moralities!

The past makes the present; the bracts protect the flower, but if the bracts persist and the blossom cannot throw them off they become throttling instruments of death.

The curse and weakness of the law is precedent, of which it boasts.

All unjust privilege is but the constipation of life. When justice refuses to flow, is dammed up by custom, and will not follow in the new channels of reason, there we find the iniquitous, stagnant pools of privilege, full of poison, parasitic lives.

What a world it would be if we could swing forward unhampered by the past!

The past is to teach us, not to bind us. It is a bane and not a blessing if it does not invigorate us to go on.

The world keeps sweet and sound, young and green, because plants die and rot, and the waters flow forever by, and institutions crumble, and old ideas fade, and Nature is strong enough to throw away continually her waste, bring us every Spring new flowers, and every Autumn new fruits.

> Swords and books and Bishops' rings!
> Fast they fall upon the pile
> Of the world's discarded things,
> A little use a little while.

THE BAPTISM

CLARICE had a baby. It was the wonder of the island. From the old fisherman down by the beach to the Honorable Joneses and Walkers up at the big hotel the baby was the subject of intense discussion. For everybody liked Clarice and her husband, who was a play-actor, and the baby was an amazing compound of the excellences of both.

Clarice wanted the baby baptized. No priest or minister could be found on the island. "Just the same, I shall have the baby baptized," said she. "I'll have Berriman do it." Berriman was a poet, past sixty, and a beautiful failure. Physically he lived on the crusts and edges of things; spiritually he ate of the heart of the world.

So one afternoon they had the christening. And Berriman, the poet, spoke, saying:

"Beloved friends, we are here gathered, in the sight of God and in the presence of these witnesses, to baptize this child.

"Baptism is the application of water to the human body, solemnly and formally, as a symbol of the cleansing of the soul. It is a most ancient rite, and is found in all religions.

"It indicates the adoption of a candidate into the membership of the elect.

"There has always been a superior few, an aristocracy in the world.

"There is the apparent or so-called aristocracy, who as a rule are not superior at all; and there is the real aristocracy, who are a secret order known to themselves only.

"We are here to baptize this baby into the real elect, the real upper-tendom, the real church, or ecclesia, or called-out.

"We therefore consecrate ourselves to teach this child to take the UPPER THOUGHT as to all things.

"To her, flowers shall not be mere plants, but God's thoughts.

"To her, stars shall be more than burning words; they shall be eyes of mystery.

"To her, men shall not be brutes, whose labor is to be exploited; they shall be brothers, prophets, spirit flames.

"To her, the sex feeling, when it comes, shall be as a lily, which, though its roots grow in common soil, yet lifts its pure petals to perfume the air, to make glad the garden, and to greet the sun.

"To her, Events shall not be as the shaking of dice, the fortuity of chance; but they shall be meaningful moves of the intelligence of destiny, which guides men and things by its own perfect plan.

"We consecrate this child to reverence and against flippancy; to justice, and against all lies; to loyalty, and against deception; to love, and against all kinds of hate; to patience, and against petulance; to beauty, and against ugliness; to greatness of mind, of heart and of soul, and to the world and the fellowship of the entire human race, against all littleness and narrowness; to the citizenship of the world and against all clans, exclusive sects, cliques and cults.

"And this little Citizen of the World and Heiress of the Future we commend unto that God who has made no thing common and to that Master who loved no less than the whole world."

THE CRY OF THE WEARY

I STOOD at one of the gates of the city where the human stream pours out to take the suburban trains. It was evening in the sky, it was evening in the faces around me, it was evening in my heart. The grimness, tenseness, mercilessness of the strife came home to me.

I waited in the railway station and saw tired, unshaven men sitting stolid or asleep from weariness; and faded women, tired, tired, tired, with insistent children tugging at their skirts, little full and strong lives devouring the weak and failing, as wolves eat their wounded.

I watched the army of workmen coming out of the factory at the closing hour, carrying dinner pails, walking with heavy, dragging feet, a few laughing as if galvanized for a moment by a joke, but the most of them looking ahead with set eyes.

I saw the mother of six when she had put the last into bed, and had sat down and seemed to collapse, as a pack-mule too heavily loaded; and she fell asleep, too tired to undress.

I saw the vaudeville actor that had been setting a thousand people into roars of laughter; he came from the stage door and his features were drawn with weariness, and his mouth wore the twisted smile of the heartbroken.

I saw the boy, alone in the city, come into his mean hall bedroom, take off his shoes as a prisoner takes off his chains, and sit with his face in his hands, too tired to go to bed.

I saw the shopgirl, when she thought no one was looking, sit down for a moment's rest, and her face was gray with exhaustion; all night long she had watched by a sickbed.

I saw a slouching man, his coat shiny, his trousers frayed; he walked stealthily into the park late at night, and sat down upon a bench; he spread a newspaper over his knees and in a moment he was asleep.

I saw the morally tired: the boy, tired of the isolation of decency, drift into the saloon and begin to drink; the girl, tired of the struggle for virtue's sake, let go and whirl away into the pool of lost souls.

And I saw strong men, betrayed and shamed, grow suddenly tired and sick of life.

And I saw old men and women tired because hope had left, enthusiasms faded, disillusion come; and they longed for the rest and peace of death.

And I saw the invalid, the broken and wounded, tired, tired, tired.

And I saw all the failures, those who were not made of stuff stern enough to win in the push and fight for success; they stood pitiful, hopeless, pathetic.

The whole world seemed to be so tired, tired, tired.

Were it not for its two friends mankind could not endure.

Its two friends are sleep and death.

THE FRIEND

A FRIEND is a person who is "for you," always, under any suspicions.

He never investigates you.

When charges are made against you, he does not ask proof. He asks the accuser to clear out.

He likes you just as you are. He does not want to alter you.

Whatever kind of coat you are wearing suits him. Whether you have on a dress suit or a hickory shirt with no collar, he thinks it's fine.

He likes your moods, and enjoys your pessimism as much as your optimism.

He likes your success. And your failure endears you to him the more.

He is better than a lover because he is never jealous.

He wants nothing from you, except that you be yourself.

He is the one being with whom you can feel SAFE. With him you can utter your heart, its badness and its goodness. You don't have to be careful.

In his presence you can be indiscreet; which means you can rest.

There are many faithful wives and husbands; there are few faithful friends.

Friendship is the most admirable, amazing, and rare article among human beings.

Anybody may stand by you when you are right; a friend stands by you even when you are wrong.

The highest known form of friendship is that of the dog to his master. You are in luck if you can find one man or one woman on earth who has that kind of affection for you and fidelity to you.

Like the shade of a great tree in the noonday heat, is a friend.

Like the home port, with your country's flag flying, after long journeys, is a friend.

A friend is an impregnable citadel of refuge in the strife of existence.

It is he that keeps alive your faith in human nature, that makes you believe it is a good universe.

He is the antidote to despair, the elixir of hope, the tonic for depression, the medicine to cure suicide.

When you are vigorous and spirited you like to take your pleasures with him; when you are in trouble you want to tell him; when you are sick you want to see him; when you are dying you want him near.

You give to him without reluctance and borrow from him without embarrassment.

If you can live fifty years and find one absolute friend you are fortunate. For of the thousands of human creatures that crawl the earth, few are such stuff as friends are made of.

THE STAIRWAY

In the house of life is a great stairway that runs from the cellar to the roof.

And I saw a hog enter the cellar and go up the stairs. As he went up he squealed and grunted, and looked for refuse to devour, but ever as he ascended his squeals turned to laughter and his grunts to sighs, and he sought bread and not filth to eat. His form also changed, so that when he had come to the upper floors he was a man, and when he reached the roof he was an angel and flew away.

And I saw also a poisonous snake, and an unclean goat, and a cruel wolf, and a surly bear, and a fierce lion, and a snarling dog, and a sneaking rat, and a wild horse, and a stupid donkey, and all manner of inhuman beasts go up, one by one, along the stairs, and at every rising step each one lost some animality and gained some humanity, and each one as he came to the top became an angel, as a chrysalis breaks into a butterfly, and flew into the sky.

And I asked: "What is this stairway of Metamorphosis that begins with the brute and ends with the superman?"

And the interpreter answered and said: "The

name of this stair, by which men climb to God, is WOMAN." The most significant thing that enters the life of man or woman is the sex feeling.

"The sex passion makes or breaks the soul.

"For ages men considered the sex lure as a device of the devil to destroy mankind. They seemed to have grounds for their belief. Thousands wallow in the bog of uncleanness, self-loathing, despair, and crime, because this powerful instinct in them is perverted. The life of the pervert is like a sixty-horsepower motor driven by a drunken chauffeur.

"Dante, with his Beatrice, showed us a better way. So also Tennyson and all the nobler poets.

"The art of nobleness consists in changing what is coarse into that which is fine, making what is common to be beautiful and strange; this can only be done by the spirit in man.

"When eating becomes communion, when washing becomes baptism, and when man-woman love becomes marriage, then they are sacraments, and life becomes sacramental and is raised from animality to high and divine level.

"Where there is nothing any more that is sacrament to man, then life sinks to the stage in which it was in the days of Augustus in Rome, which Matthew Arnold described:

> "On that hard pagan world disgust
> And secret loathing fell;
> Deep weariness and sated lust
> Made human life a hell."

THE CAGE

A GIRAFFE in the Paris Zoo has broken his head against the bars of his cage. What ailed the beast? For seventeen years he has had plenty of fodder and drink, an attendant in uniform and gold lace to wait on him, and the privilege of making the crowd gape. It was a career each of us is dying for. It would seem that Mr. Giraffe was hard to please.

When you go to a circus you see not only the caged brutes in the menagerie, but around the sawdust ring you find little wooden-fenced inclosures; in these sit the elect. Similar cages are at the prize fight, the roof garden, and the horse show. Nobody is IT unless he has a fence around him.

Then there are the boxes at the theatre, the very worst places in the house from which to see what is going on upon the stage. But when you put a barrier around the poorest seats you can charge for them three times the price of good seats.

The only reason we want money is that we may buy a cage. As soon as a man gets rich he procures a house with a yard and a high iron fence around it. If a visitor enters the yard and gets by the bulldog he still has difficulty in breaking into the mansion. A butler meets him at the door to see if his clothes look fit, and a secretary meets him in the hall to make sure he is not after money.

When a woman acquires money her one desire also is to find a cage. She yearns for exclusiveness. Her altitude in the social scale is measured by the number of persons she will not speak to.

What we call getting up in the world amounts to getting properly caged. We want to travel in a private car—at least, in a private compartment. We want our meals at the hotel served in our own private dining room. We want to be shaved by our own private valet and not in the barber shop. Anything to be caged off from the people.

The instinct is in us from the first. Turn a child loose in a garden. What birds and insects he cannot kill he captures and wants to cage.

When we say a woman loves birds we mean she has one or more poor little wild things hanging in cages around the house.

You may find here and there a squirrel in a cage; to give him exercise and to amuse him an infernal wheeled grill has been arranged in which the captive travels miles; he doubtless enjoys it —about as much as you would enjoy a treadmill; his mistress "loves animals."

Meanwhile there remain a few souls who really love freedom. They decline to "belong" to all sorts of things. They refuse to be bound by convention and the opinions of other people. They don't want to get away from the common people, but to know and love them better. They love flowers and have no desire to pick them. They love birds—in trees and hedgerows. They love wild beasts—in the woods, and have no desire to see them pacing up and down in cages. They want to be free, free, free. And they want all other people to be free.

Some of these are tramps. Some are the caged captives of convention sighing through the bars. Some are poets, like Whitman, crying:

"I utter my barbaric yawp over the roofs of the world."

THE BLESSING

In the days of our youth the family never sat down to the table without the blessing. All heads would be bowed, and all the clatter of child-voices would hush, while father would say:

"For what we are about to receive, O Lord, make us truly grateful. Amen."

Alas! the blessing is gone. Nobody gets up to breakfast, or the affair is a "movable feast," where one at a time the people appear, snatch a bite and a sup and hurry away.

There are even many who have their coffee and rolls while lying abed; of which custom let us say nothing.

City people eat their midday meal downtown in restaurant or club, where, of course, there is no room for blessing—quite the contrary.

The family usually gathers at dinner, but in how many households do they fall to, like unsouled animals, without one word of grace to redeem the crassness of feeding?

I hold it is not a matter of belonging to a church, believing a creed, or professing to be pious, but that it is an act of decency, and of human dignity, and of that spiritual self-respect all souls ought to have to say grace.

Adopt the custom in your household. Let there be at least one minute in the day when, as a family, officially and ritually, you seriously recognize that you are children of the infinite, pensioners upon the bounty of "a power not of yourselves."

Don't let your peculiar theology, or lack of it, hinder you from a sweet and wholesome ceremony that may light up a sordid day with a little beam of the Sun of souls.

One family I know used to sing the blessing; and who, whether Jew, Buddhist, Christian, or agnostic, could be anything but bettered by joining for a moment, before eating, in this hymn?

> "Be present at our table, Lord;
> Be here as everywhere adored;
> Feed us with bread, and grant that we
> May feast in paradise with Thee!"

If that sounds too churchly, say the quaint "Selkirk Grace," once used by Bobby Burns:

> "Some hae meat and canna eat,
> And some wad eat that want it,
> But we hae meat, and we can eat,
> And sae the Lord be thanket!"

Think! Here we all are, fellow travellers, upon "the good ship Earth," whirling through starry ways. We know not whence we came nor whither we go. We know not our appointed time. There is some power, some mind, in the sum of things, that has all these secrets.

Eating should be the sacrament indicative of our reasonable reverence for that Supreme Guiding Spirit.

Say this grace of Robert Louis Stevenson, liberal enough for all, to whatever power you believe in:

"Help us to repay in service one to another the debt of Thine unmerited benefits and mercies."

THE CITY AND PRIVACY

ONE reason why people flock to cities is that they may be able to mind their own business.

Political economists seek complex and devious reasons for the tremendous rapidity of city growth and for the desertion of the country and of the country town. The cause, however, is quite simple, as simple as human nature. The people go to cities because they "want to." That's all.

Take the village of Podunk. In the first place you would not be allowed to go there to live without explaining why you came, where you came from, and what your business is. You can rent a flat in Chicago, however, and nobody cares a tuppence who you are or what is your criminal record, so long as you are peaceable.

If you do business in Podunk, and usually get down to the store at nine, and some morning you do not appear until ten, the town will not rest until it has found out the cause of your delay.

Your neighbors know all about you and your wife, your sons, and your daughters. The bank cashier knows the size of your pile, the grocer and butcher know what you eat, the dry goods merchant knows what sort of underclothes you wear and how much your women folks spend on corsets, and they all meet and check up.

When you leave town they know it, also when you return; and they want to know what you were doing in St. Louis.

It is all a very cosy family arrangement. You live in the constant glare of the limelight.

Some people like it, and feel lost and lonesome in the city. But more and more that class is growing to whom this perpetual invasion of privacy is disagreeable.

It is pretty generally assumed among moralists that people love the privacy of cities because they wish to plunge into vice. Doubtless some do. But it is doubtful if the average city-bred person is any more immoral than the country-bred.

It is conceivable that a person may wish to live his own life as he pleases, and not under the unremitting supervision of Mrs. Grundy, and that this wish may be prompted not by a desire for secret crime but simply by a desire for personal privacy.

The matter is really a conflict between the old idea that morality is conformity and the modern idea that morality is the responsible expression of one's own personality.

The city means the revolt of the soul of man against moral dictation. Of course, wicked people have always resented moral tyranny. Now the good people are beginning to resent it too. So the country is squeezing out its best and its worst into the cities.

A WEALTHY MAN

I have received a remarkable letter. It is so significant that I am going to give the greater part of it, amended a bit, to my readers.

Here is a man, it seems to me, who has got himself on the right side of the universe. He is so rich he makes me ashamed of my poverty. He writes:

"I am very wealthy.

"Although you will look in vain for my name in 'Who's Who' or the society 'Blue Book,' nevertheless all the art treasures of Mr. Morgan or Mr. Altman are trifles compared to my possessions.

"As I write I glance at one of them in rapt admiration and wonder. It is an inexhaustible source of delight to me. Its gifts to me are so prolific that I can trample them under foot, yet still they come.

"My gems are beyond price. The pleasure they supply to me is unalloyed, for they give me no worry along with their enjoyment. I have no fear of burglars. Whoso would rob me would but enrich me further.

"All this vast wealth is confined within the

small area of a few hundred feet of the earth's surface, a portion of ground for which I have toiled the greater part of my fifty years of life.

"The thing of beauty I refer to is a noble SUGAR MAPLE TREE about sixty or seventy feet high, in all the glory of its autumnal foliage.

"To-day it is vermilion and green and gold in the sunlight after a drenching rain.

"Every leaf is a jewel, and every one different, thousands upon thousands of them. No rare enamels can compare with them. They shame the porcelains of China, the vases of Japan, the king's treasures from Dresden or Sevres.

"The delicate tracery, the fantastic shapes, the tumult of color in these leaves! They are full of the craftsmanship-joy, the artist-delight, of the infinite Creator. I feel by the joy I get in appreciating them what joy He must have in making them.

"They are falling one by one, and lie in splotches of rich color upon the green of the grass, which flashes with raindrops in all the hues of the prism, a carpet of oriental colors upon a background of diamonds.

"And when all the leaves have returned to the earth from which they came, where they will help to fertilize new lives, I will still have my Tree to admire. Its beautiful naked limbs will be etched against the sky, its rugged bark upon its sturdy trunk will hide the inner secret of life to come.

"I get rest from my Tree, and high thoughts, and winged fancies, which I cannot utter.

"I see two things in my Maple, the two things which speak to my soul, and whisper to me the secret of the world and of the world to come, and of all worthy living.

"The two things are STRENGTH AND BEAUTY."

THE FIREPLACE

In the modern dwelling the fireplace has disappeared, the steam radiator has been substituted.

The change is not without significance to the spirits of men. The fire on the hearth was the symbol of THE FAMILY. It was the original altar, the centre about which gathered the first human institution.

In the advance ranks of "progress" The Family is likewise vanishing. A certain group of futurist thinkers, typified by H. G. Wells, seriously propose the State instead of The Family as the proper agent to care for children.

We move from flat to flat, like gypsies. Our children are born at stations by the way, and have no home feeling.

Divorces increase; for women are travelling companions, not home makers.

By our most praiseworthy charities we are undermining The Family. By many of those schemes, both of Church and State, by which we seek to "save" the individual, we try to do what ought to be done through The Family.

Old ladies are put into institutional homes,

often, when it is the duty and the blessing of The Family to keep them.

The children of the well-to-do, who ought to be growing up in daily contact with mother, father, brothers, and sisters, are sent away to private schools. They may get expert training, but they miss that family life that is infinitely more valuable to them, and equally as necessary to the parents.

Babies will be taken care of by hospitals, foundling asylums, and other charitable institutions, provided the mother will renounce all claim to her offspring.

We heal defective souls and bodies and rescue the perishing generally, but we insist upon suppressing the function of The Family. The mother is incompetent, the father unfit, the environment is unideal; hence, take the child away to a huge brick barracks where he can be herded scientifically with other children.

Rational helpfulness should aid the defective individual by aiding The Family. For The Family is more important than the individual.

It is more to be desired that we maintain The Family than that we preserve the Nation or the Church.

Without Family life we are what Urbain Gohier calls "une poussiere de peuples," a dust-people, loose grains of sand, with no solidarity.

The "live your own life" gospel is often dangerously near humbuggery. Every young man and young woman should plan to have children, born in happy marriage, growing up in an atmosphere of Family love; for there is nothing that so develops one's soul as the responsibilities, the joys, and sorrows of The Family. by Eva

We need a deal of wholesome human feeling to resist the entirely corrupting influence of artificial mantels over artificial grates where there is no fire, or at least but a gas log, and of radiators, and of registers, holes in the floors where hot air comes up. Would that there were some way to gather The Family once more around blazing logs and a hearthstone!

For the most beautiful cross in the world is composed of two sticks crossed and burning in the fireplace, with father, mother, and the children all gathered around it.

The Family is the first spiritual unit of mankind, the real Church, "and the gates of hell shall not prevail against it." underlined by Eva

Oh how I have always wanted a fireplace + candles Eva

THE SAND PILE

SOME men the other day came around and dumped about forty wagon loads of sand in the street at our corner. They are going to use it in repaving the street; but meanwhile it is being put to a far better use.

For, as soon as the heap was complete, out from all sorts of places came small children and covered the sand heap, even as flies come and cover a lump of sugar.

I can see them out of my window now, and hear them; for they are shrieking like mad, as all children do who are having a perfectly gorgeous time.

If I could tell you all that is happening on that sand it would make more interesting reading than a pageful of newspaper crimes or a bookful of Diamond Dick adventures.

Over there a pirate has captured a crew of merchantmen and made them walk the plank. One by one the poor wretches tumbled down the sand, while the bold Captain Kidd with his sword of lath stood mercilessly at the top.

A general has led his troops to glory. He is an Irish boy of seven; his army consists of his two sisters and two neighbor boys. But it was a famous victory. They liked it so well they did it over and over.

There have been knife fights on the cliff, terrific struggles with the Indians, bloody hold-ups, prize fights, and bear fights.

Little Sissy Matthews, aged three, has rolled down the sand mountain until she is half sand herself; and her soul is filled with pure joy, even as her ears are filled with sand.

They have dug holes, moulded forts, made houses, pierced tunnels. They have patted the sand and piled it and thrown it and rolled in it, everything but eaten it.

On behalf of the children I wish to thank the municipality for its kind consideration. Whether the street needs paving or not I will not undertake to discuss, but it is certain that the children need all the laughter and glee that is contained in that sand pile.

Therefore, O wise and learned rulers of the town, I would petition you to come on with the sand. Please make some more heaps. Dump one at every corner.

It is good of you to provide schools where the little ones can sit up straight and study and not whisper. But oh! how much more bliss and rapture in a hill of sand!

All day long thousands of children stay in their cooped-up flats, or go out to play in streets crowded with murderous automobiles and trucks.

So that a sand pile is a godsend, and goes toward realizing the prophecy of the seer of old:

"And the streets of the city shall be full of boys and girls playing in the streets thereof."

MUSIC

THE study of music should be made compulsory in the public schools.

The whole populace should be taught what true music is. The only way to accomplish this is to cause the children continually to hear, to sing, and to perform upon instruments music of the highest quality.

Cheap and nasty music is worse than cheap and nasty meat and bread; the former destroys the character, the latter only the body.

The average popular music of America to-day is without doubt the most base and evil ever in the world. It is without ingenuity, taste, or musical value. It is as injurious as profanity. The wretched tunes are more deleterious than the smut-words to which they are set.

A generation of boys and girls brought up on Bach, Beethoven, Gounod, and Wagner would have souls 100 per cent. higher in quality than the unfortunate children of to-day fed upon ragtime and melodies of contemptible inanity.

The greatest danger threatening this nation is that it may become utterly material and trivial; for triviality invariably accompanies materialism and the decay of ideals.

A nation that has no deep-hearted songs, a nation that can not or will not sing, can be no organic thing; it is but loose dust.

The most terrible trait of the laborers of the United States is not their violence nor their drink, but the fact that they do not sing at their meetings.

Cultured and well-to-do people have a tendency to perversion and idle mischief because there is no music in them. Who ever heard of a fashionable "function" where the guests sang choruses and part-songs?

Our people are educated to have music made AT them, not to make music themselves; a fatal, deadly mistake.

The American cabaret is a ghastly and, to an intelligent person, a most boresome affair. Watch the hideous, wriggling women and jumping males trying to entertain the eaters and drinkers, who sit with stolid, cheerless faces!

A company of German students in a beer cellar is jovial, because they can sing, and sing music that has worth.

Not the least reason why the church is losing its hold upon the masses is that congregations have ceased to sing. A company of worshippers that hire their music to be performed before them is already dead.

There can be no civic conscience, no clean politics, no firm organization of the people, without music as a basis. Those who cannot sing together cannot act together for high spiritual and political ends.

Music is not an entertainment, an accomplishment, a side-show.

It is as necessary for the populace to have music as they march toward their civic and national goals as it is for an army to have bands or to chant folk-hymns on its way to battle.

A dumb democracy is a dead one.

We are the dumb slaves of such organizations as Tammany because we do not sing; for those who have no music in their souls cannot keep step.

Why quarrel over teaching religion in the public schools? Why not teach music, which is the gist of all religions? "It is incontestable," says M. Victor de Laprade, a French writer on music, "that music induces in us a sense of the infinite and the contemplation of the invisible."

"See deep enough," says Carlyle, "and you see musically; the heart of Nature being everywhere music."

And William Watson:

> Nay, what is Nature's
> Self, but an endless
> Strife towards music,
> Euphony, rhyme?

We must learn as a people to love good music, or we shall perish of sheer cheapness and shallowness of soul.

NO NEED OF CHARM

In "The Marriage Game," Mrs. Flexner's play, occurs a fine line:

"Unless a woman wants something she has no business to want, she has no need of charm."

No need of charm! How many a foolish little brain, devoid of understanding, has shipwrecked things by this unreason!

The silly woman, who exerted all her arts and wiles to draw a suitor, drops her efforts with him become a husband. Her market's made. She has caught her train, is safely aboard, and why run any more?

She gives frank expression to her peevish whims and ailments. She is captious, critical.

She is dowdy at breakfast. She is unkempt and sloppily dressed when they two are alone.

Exert one's self to woo a husband? Why, there are those women who seem to think it's hardly decent.

And right here is the cue for the entrance of "the other woman."

Many a man, too, thinks the game's up when he has haltered and altared the woman of his choice. The excitement of the chase is over. It's "married and done for."

Then if the woman be strongly human, as she generally is, and a bit weak and sensitive, as she often is, marriage breaks down. Possibly—enter "the other man."

People speak of having tried marriage and found it a failure. Most of them have not tried at all. That is the trouble. They didn't "try."

Eternal vigilance is the price of love, as well as of liberty. Success, in marriage also, means keeping everlastingly at it.

To sit down, once married, and expect to be coddled, waited on, served, and pleased, you a king on a throne and your mate your servitor, is rather sure to bring on swift ruin.

There is not one wife in a thousand that could not keep her husband if she would keep working at the job. The wife has a thousand advantages over the other woman.

And if a husband will only not stop making love he need fear no rival.

Most of the unhappy marriages are due to selfishness plus pure boneheadedness.

The love and devotion of a good woman, and of an honest man, is worth working hard for.

And the beauty of it is that it is the most delightful work in the world, once it gets established as a habit.

You need charm every day you live.

THE PRACTICE OF GREATNESS BY WORDS

You take exercises for the muscles of your arms, legs, and back; why not take an exercise occasionally for your soul?

Your spirit, or ego, or self, or whatever you may call that inner invisible something that is more really you than your body; that something which thinks, loves, feels, imagines, and wills is well worth a little training.

Here is a suggestion. There are certain great ideas, represented by certain great words. These words have power-volts in their very sound. Every time you think one of them you grow greater.

Take to bed with you the following seven words. As you lie, waiting for sleep, say them over, one by one, to yourself.

Or, better, take a half hour during the day, in silence and solitude, and practise the feeling of these terms.

God. Never mind about your belief or disbelief. Say that word ten times, slowly, with pauses between. Think of what is above, below, around, and in all things. Spread your mind out upon the universe. Practise the sensing of the infinite.

STARS. Say Stars. Think Stars. Try to reach the feeling of stars. Let your fancy climb to the top of the night sky. Get the vibrations of those measureless distances, those suns, galaxies, sweeping worlds; all silent, luminous, immense, swift whirling yet orderly. Happy you if you can induce a bit of star feeling within you!

MOUNTAIN. Repeat some names of individuals; Mont Blanc, Himalaya, Orizaba, Matterhorn, Popocatepetl. Get your mind up among the noiseless heights. Let the serenity, the eternity of the words filter into you.

OCEAN. Go a-sailing, out of sight of land. Be surrounded for a moment by waste, wild waters. See on all sides only horizon. Stand, in your imagination, by the seashore. Hear the surf boom. Do not talk. Do not make phrases. Feel!

TREE. Call to mind the most majestic tree you know. Touch its rough trunk. Look up at its wide branches. Stand from it and see its outline against the sky. Get some of the Tree feeling into your spirit. Think Trees; it's a wonderful relief from thinking dishes and dust-rags.

DAWN. Think of sunrise, of the freshness of life, of hopeful beginnings. Induce, if you can, a sense of sunrise.

MORE. It is a sonorous word. Repeat it—slowly, significantly, and note how you grow. The word lifts you up, expands you.

Don't try to argue. Just say these seven words.

Let them boom across your consciousness. Somehow they will still and banish your littleness. You will come to a great calm. You will have a sense of poise. You will get a sense of remoteness from affairs. You cannot describe it, nor impart it. It is a secret.

Your self-contempt will vanish. You will cease to think yourself a nothing, a puppet, insignificant.

You will feel that you are, deep in your hidden life, great and strong and wonderful. For who can think such thoughts and be wholly little and contemptible?

WHAT WE CAN NEVER KNOW

THE most striking thing about a really learned man is not the extent of his knowledge, but the extent of his admitted ignorance. The wiser a person is the greater the number of things he doesn't know.

The more universally cock-sure and well informed one seems the more likely it is that he is a humbug.

> Socrates . . .
> Whom well inspir'd the oracle pronounced
> Wisest of men,

used often to say he knew nothing.

How little has science made inroad upon that stupendous and limitless nescience that surrounds it, as the stellar universe enfolds the tiny earth!

Sir Oliver Lodge the other day, at the meeting of the British Association, spoke of the mystery of sex determination. Spite of all claims, we know little more to-day than did the cave men why one child is born a boy and another a girl, and why the world ratio keeps about the same.

Sir Oliver also expressed his wonder that some plants bore both male and female flowers. He said the same sap comes into the stem, but just at that junction where differently sexed flowers branched away from each other there must be some profound change in the sap.

"I don't know what it is, and microscopes tell me nothing about it," he continued. "Perhaps if physiologists could find out just what happens in that little plant joint they would get some clue to the reason why some human beings are born boys and others girls."

He might have pushed further his point of wonder. How comes it that the earth juices make here a white flower and there a red? How is a huge oak all folded in a little acorn?

How can nature make the peach, full of juice and cased so closely in the thinnest of fuzzy skin that never leaks?

How does blood food here create a hard finger-nail, there a hair, and there a stony tooth?

What is electricity? We know somewhat of how it acts. But what is it? We know little more of it than does a savage.

What is life? What is that secret force that transforms in a trice a living dog, who eats his environment, into a dead dog, whose environment eats him?

What is love? Why does this woman thrill you and that one leave you cold or repel you?

What is conscience, that world's policeman that

urges us on to what we think right and affrights us at what we think wrong?

What is truth? What is personality? What is being?

And these questions are not remote, academic questions, not such things as Huxley called "lunar politics," but they touch the very nearest and dearest regions of every man's life.

We are but dust-motes in the sunbeam of the infinite. We cling like oysters to our little point in the bed of the vast ocean of mystery.

All about us is nature, deep-wombed, gray-eyed, her mind a galaxy of secrets, her thoughts far and strange as the procession of the suns.

Nothing befits us, her children, so much as reverence for her purposes, humility before her great brain, trust and love in her vast heart.

No one is so consummate an ass as the one who thinks he knows it all.

"AND NO ONE SHALL WORK FOR MONEY"

It is usually put forth as a knockdown argument that if men did not have to work for bread and butter they would not work at all.

It is assumed as a matter of course that money is the representative of the only universal motive of human energy, and that if all were assured a good living nobody would turn a hand.

I do not believe this. I believe that money is not a legitimate motive at all. To illustrate, let us imagine that state of the world, to which we will come some day, where wages exist no more.

Let us suppose we have so developed the state that every child is assured of care and due training. No ignorant, unskilled, or criminally defective beings are brought into the number of independent adults. If incapable of decent life on arriving at manhood they are taken care of in proper institutions.

Let us suppose also that every person is fed, housed, and clothed by the state. No man or woman needs to labor to make a living. The entire motive of subsistence is eliminated.

Instead of this resulting in the paralysis of all

energy, it would be but the beginning of progress. As Moryd Sheridan says: "When our existence is comfortably assured, the battle of life will have begun in earnest."

Men, with their present stock of ideals, would of course drop into idleness under such circumstances; but men now differ from men then almost as much as a hog differs from a man. It is frankly to be admitted that altruistic feelings and civic conscience must be greatly strengthened. Conditions now are the only practical ones for half-barbarous creatures such as we are at present.

But let us be specific. What motives precisely will supersede personal gain?

Instead of work for money there will be craftsmanship for the joy of it. People now love to make, do, and manage things, for fun, when the things are what they enjoy doing. The problem of civilization is to change labor into craft, and thus into play.

Machinery is more and more replacing the drudgery of hands. The steam dredger does the work of a hundred hand shovels; carry that on a hundred years and imagine the vast amount of disagreeable effort that will be taken from men.

There will be the enthusiasms of art, of music, of letters and science. Even now the best work here is not at all for money and is poorly paid.

The joy of home making is not a money-paid pleasure. The wives and mothers of the future will be as busy and as happy as now.

We are all sensitive to public opinion. The scorn of our fellows is a sharp whip. As we progress it will grow sharper. Men will be ASHAMED TO BE IDLE. Human beings work as hard to avoid contempt as to get money. To have the esteem and praise of the community will move men as powerfully as to make gain.

In a wage-free democracy we shall not only have better poems and paintings and scientific discoveries and music, but street cars will be run better, groceries and milk will be of better quality and better distributed, meals will be better cooked, clothes will be better made, and all the little, necessary work of the world better done, because always a large part of the people can do these things and cannot write poetry nor compose music.

You remember Tom Sawyer's getting the boys to whitewash his fence, when he made it SEEM FUN to them?

That is plain human nature. And I believe all men will do more and better work when they shall work because it is fun to them, and when not to work will only mean the contempt of their fellows.

And, take it now, the people who never have to care for bread or clothing are about as energetic as the farm-hands, with, of course, notable exceptions among the perverts of society and of "society's" hangers on.

THE SCHOOL YARD

Few greater wrongs can be done an American child than to deprive him of the privilege of the Public School.

I am not so sure children get much training in the schoolhouse that really trains, for we are still monstrously medieval with our "grades," "courses of study," and "examinations," classifying human beings like cabbages, pigeon-holing them and working them through systems as if they were scientific specimens, instead of studying them and developing the singular talent in each of them.

But there is no doubt as to the educational value of the school playground. It is there that your little darling will learn that one thing he needs to know above and before all other things, to wit: Democracy.

It is there he will get the self-conceit punched out of him. He will learn to play the man. He will learn self-reliance, courage, and "not to think more highly of himself than he ought to think."

Children, even the offspring of snobs and snobesses, are natural born democrats. They know no distinction of race, creed, or social position.

Your child will play with the little Chinese boy and never dream he is not a perfectly good human being until you teach him.

Sir Francis Vane of Hutton, in the September number of the *Contemporary Review,* tells how, when he had established a school in the Transvaal, the little whites and blacks studied and sported together in entire good will, until the Dutch parents begged him as a favor not to allow their children to play with colored ones.

He continues: "I have seen this fight of the young for freedom from race and caste prejudice, against elderly sinners—the laggards of time—not in one country, but in many. In Italy on the democratic sands of Viareggio, where Shelley died, I have seen little people playing in harmony together, and suddenly separated by those whose duty it was to instil wisdom and Christianity into them with these words: 'I will not have you play with Protestant children.' I have seen at San Sebastian children educated in the vulgarity of class prejudice just as I have in race; and I can never forget my own first experience in this kind of stupid cruelty, when as a child of nine I had played with a small girl of the same age one long morning, and she, having been invited to our house to dinner, to my surprise and mortification was sent to the kitchen for her meal while I had mine in solitary state in the day nursery. To my vehement inquiry why we should be divided, the governess's reply was, 'But you are a little gentleman'—a poor and inexplicable consolation for having my food alone!"

For some time to come, doubtless, grown-ups will continue their vulgar, Pharisaic, and septic notions and practices of class prejudice; but something should be done to save the little ones.

Parents should realize that no more dangerous idea can get itself fixed in the child mind than that he is of a class apart from and superior to ordinary people; or that there are insuperable barriers between high-born and low-born, rich and poor, white and yellow, Hebrew and Christian.

Georg Ebers describes a saint in Mount Sinai who crawled into a hole, away from the wicked world, but when they found him dead they found also that he had written upon the wall that famous line of Terence, "Homo sum; humani nihil a me alien puto." (I am a man, and I consider nothing human alien to me.)

No institution for the inculcation of the sense of humanity has ever been devised that is better than the United States public school yard.

THE CURSE OF POVERTY

THERE is but one calamity—poverty. There is but one thing to be desired—riches.

Any kind of poverty is bad: material, intellectual, emotional, spiritual.

Every bodily disease is due to bodily poverty: of the blood, of nutrition, of elimination, of co-ordination.

Malignant germs abound everywhere. But they are snobs. They do not attack the rich-blooded, the richly functioned; they pounce upon the anemic. A health-rich boy can have a million pneumonia microbes in his mouth and not be hurt.

Money poverty is bad. You do not have to be a money worshipper to believe that you cannot lead a decent life without income enough to get you comfortable clothing, wholesome food, a sanitary habitation, and the saving bits of culture and leisure.

It is perfectly right for us to want money enough to secure a reasonable independence. Any one who is not investing regularly a portion of his earnings is a fool. Thrift is just as sterling a virtue now as it was in the days of Ben Franklin. Any child not trained to save is wronged.

The newspapers are full of the news of domestic scandal. It is due to poverty of love, and poverty of character.

The richest rich people on earth are they who have plenty of love.

And how terrible and far-reaching are the effects of mind poverty!

The people are like "dumb, driven cattle," herded by shrewd political bosses. Their children are stunted, their homes are cramped, their rights are denied them, their food is poisoned, they are insulted, despised, pillaged, and swindled, simply because they are ignorant, they are victims of intellectual poverty, they don't know what to do.

Duly train just one generation of children and see what a tremendous silent revolution would ensue!

It is the great army of the ignorant who stir up violence, follow fatuous enthusiasms and bring defeat in the battles of the people.

It is the moral poverty of the money-rich that renders them pests.

It is the spiritual poverty of the Church that makes it ineffective.

It is the artistic poverty of the People that gives us ugly cities, dreary streets, stuffy flats, hideous advertising plastered over street cars and billboards.

It is artistic poverty that produces poor theatrical shows, wretched, musically poverty-stricken comic operas, idea-poverty-stricken plays.

It is moral impotence that causes the dearth of honest men as great leaders.

Yet reformers hawk preventive remedies. Prohibit this, stop that, curb the other! Humanity needs the bit, the brake, and the restraint of its too powerful forces!

Stuff and nonsense! The one thing mankind needs is more force, more fire, more steam, more riches.

Never more than now. Democracy needs a thousandfold more money than royalty. Freedom needs more brains than serfdom. Virtue needs more energy than vice. Love is aseptic in proportion as it is potent. Real religion is only in surcharged souls; watery and timid souls can have but Pharisaism.

Give us riches! Rich hearts to love mightily, rich brains to think boldly, rich hands to work skilfully, rich bodies to live wholesomely, riches of culture to keep us out of the bogs of barbarism, riches of music, of sculpture, of architecture, riches of spirit to grasp the majesty of moral laws, and riches of money to secure our personal independence.

The great man is the man of full life.

"And he shall be like a tree planted by the rivers of water, that bringeth forth fruit; his leaf also shall not wither; and whatsoever he doeth shall prosper."

WHAT IS BEST?

WHAT is the best? We all agree we should strive for it, but what is it? Christians say the answer is found in the Bible, Mahometans in the Koran, some say it is in the theories of Herbert Spencer, others of Descartes.

These have been given as "the greatest good": righteousness, happiness, wisdom, love, holiness, and so on.

My own notion is that "the best" is whatever favors the fullest development of the personality. I believe we are set in this garden of the world to grow, and that he who grows most perfectly is the best man.

There are in us sensual, selfish, and other so-called "evil" qualities, and others called "higher" elements or "good." What is the difference?

The evil elements are those which the experience of the race has shown to be destructive, their pleasure is brief; the higher are those proven to be both lasting in themselves and preservative and strengthening to the whole man.

Over the individual man is mankind. From this comes a still truer fact. Whatever is hostile to the full development and permanent order, health, and joy of the whole race becomes a "bad" thing for the single person; and whatever promotes the welfare of humanity is a "good" in the one man.

From this comes what we call morality, which is the limiting of the individual self-expression by the collective. I may have an impulse to gluttonize, steal, or kill; if I and all others freely indulged such promptings the race would be imperilled; hence they are "wicked."

The moralities therefore are not the inventions of priests, are not forms of tyranny. No man nor conspiracy could establish a fake or artificial system of ethics which will stand the test of time. For morals are the feeling of self-preservation in the race, superimposed upon the feeling of self-expression in the individual.

The great "law-givers" never "gave" laws at all. They discovered them. They were poets, seers. Moses discovered the Ten Commandments; he perceived them to be the real principles of racial self-preservation. Socrates, Buddha, Confucius and all the sages merely saw vast race-principles and gave them to us as correctives of individual forces.

Let us go back to our definition, "the best is whatever favors the fullest growth of the personality," and ask how we may know what this is. The answer is, by experience, not only individual experience, but the experience of the whole world.

The latter is stored in our conscience, cellared in our inborn sense of right and wrong.

The man who pursues only self-expression, and gives self up to sensual, intellectual, or spiritual self-indulgence, is a dangerous man. He is surely headed for tragedy.

But the man who, while freely indulging every instinct, every desire, yet feels in himself a race-consciousness that controls his private impulses, such a man is truly altruistic.

When altruism becomes a passion we call it religion.

Thus, then, we may know what is "best." First, it is whatever in us seeks expression, it is the forthputting of our personality. And second, it is the world-consciousness, more or less manifested in love, patriotism, God, and all inclusive race-passions, guiding and fostering our individual desires.

I know that hope, faith, courage, and chaste-mindedness are good because I feel that if all the world practised them it would be well. I know that fear, pride, petulance, greed, and such things are bad, because if everybody were governed by such emotions it would produce chaos and universal unhappiness. This is practically Kant's "categorical imperative." It is a simple, understandable means of deciding by common-sense, and not by authority nor hearsay, what is "best."

A CHRISTMAS CARD

My Dear Friend—Christmas is coming, the great human festival. It is making me realize as it approaches that the best possessions I have been able to get from life are my friendships.

I want to give something to my friends.

The other night, after thinking it all over, I was surprised by the old truth, which came strongly to me, that what friends want most is to know we think of them and love them.

Therefore I am going just to tell you I think of you, that Christmas to me means you, that you are a part of the spirit of these times in my life.

I want to tell you that the thought of you is sunshine to me. When memory brings back our days and words together, I am glad.

If I were Fate I should make you very happy. I should write success upon your hands and brain every day, and bring restful sleep to you every night. Each impulse from my heart goes out to you in well-wishing.

I like you. And I am angry with the space that separates us and the circumstances that render our meetings few. You are "my kind of folks," and I have a constant desire to be near you.

I do not believe any of us realize how much friends mean to us, how their spirits subtly touch and stimulate ours when we are far apart, and what a glorious companionship they make for us when their faces gather around us in fancy in our moments of loneliness. Your face, my friend, is often with me, and I wish you could know what cheer it always brings.

So here's to you! I raise the glass of memory brimful of happy recollections and drink to you.

All my good wishes fly to you as doves. I appreciate what you have meant to me. I value your personality, just as it is. I clasp your hand through the intervening distance. From the bottom of my heart I say "God bless you!"

I think of you when I recall these words of Goethe:

"This world is so waste and empty, when we figure but towns and hills and rivers in it; but to know that some one is living on with us, even in silence, this makes our earthly ball a peopled garden."

WHAT IS A WOMAN TO DO?

An anonymous letter has come to my desk. As a rule such missives slide right over into the waste-basket. But this one is different. It is not a cowardly effort to stab, nor malicious, nor in any wise the ordinary anonymous nuisance. It is so human, so real, and so gives expression to a very vital and common problem that I will make some quotation from it.

After a few observations upon my writings which modesty prevents me from here setting forth, the writer says:

"Briefly, my problem is a very old one, merely that of a woman who has long suffered from intense loneliness and heart-hunger. My greatest need seems to be the love and companionship of a congenial man.

"I am well born, coming from an old family of refinement, culture, and one-time wealth. I am also well educated, a graduate of one of our foremost women's colleges. I am no longer young, neither am I old; my friends flatter me by saying that I look ten years younger than I am. Always have I had the reputation of unusual charm, that of personality, perhaps, rather than of beauty.

"How, please, is a woman alone, without family—for all have died—and with no social background to meet desirable men, in a great city? Such a one would like to make friends and comrades from among whom she could find a suitable mate. With every possible advantage of education and culture, living in a delightfully artistic home, adapted in every way to offer hospitality to friends, I perforce live practically the life of a hermit.

"Is it any wonder that we restless, unsatisfied women, whom nature has intended for wives and mothers, should seek some avenue for expression, some absorbing interest which will enable us to stifle our longings?

"Politics, or any sort of a career of publicity, does not appeal to me. I want a home and children.

"Is it that there are no men of my kind in the city? And if there aie such, why is it so impossible to meet them?

"A well-known physician recently observed that 'city men are not marrying men.' It is a great pity.

"Boy and man friends I have had all my life, but never has the right one come. Perhaps, as has been said of me, I am too exclusive, too much inclined to seek the ideal. Certainly the tricks of such as 'Annie' in Shaw's 'Man and Superman' I have never felt I could stoop to.

"What can a refined woman do, who believes

in marriage and the family, and who has scorned the occupation of husband-hunting? It seems to be too often the other type of woman who wins the man.

"Pardon me if I do not sign my name. How can I to such a letter as this?"

I cannot answer this appeal, for the simple reason that I do not know the answer. I give the letter to you, gentle reader, that you may realize, as this epistle so strongly impressed it upon me, that there are situations in life which our present civilization, morals, and conventions do not touch. Monogamy, religion, society's customs are good enough and suit the many, but they are far from covering all of the deep needs and peculiar issues of the human heart.

And how pitiful our little smug philosophy before this primeval cry of human instinct!

Lady Unknown, I can only, through the darkness, send you a sincere thought, a handclasp of sympathy, and offer up a prayer to the kindly fates that they may send you, some adventurous day, your Prince and Knight, who shall know and value your woman's worth. I will not be like the father in Tennyson,

> "With a little hoard of maxims
> Preaching down a daughter's heart."

SHOULD GIRLS PAY?

SPEAKING of the emancipation of woman and all that, there is one little item that seems to be overlooked. In order to get upon the same footting as man, the woman demands the vote, the right to be a police officer, and to sit on a jury, the privilege of being a lawyer, physician, preacher, and merchant, commercial traveller, author, and clerk, and the eligibility to carry the latch-key.

One thing is passed by in the strife of tongues. It is the right of the woman to pay.

Reference is here had more particularly to young women in re food and drink, taxicabs, carfare, ice cream sodas, dances, and theatres.

Think, sisters! So long as custom demands that you allow the male to settle the bill at the restaurant when you have consumed ten dollars' worth of birds and vintage, while he has had milk toast, on the plea of indigestion, but for the real reason of impecuniosity, will you not always be upon the level of an inferior, a child, a slave?

Can a girl retain her self-esteem when she permits her masculine escort to count out the ten cents for her chocolate sundae at the drug store, as if forsooth she were some sort of canary—let us not say poodle—to be fed with dainties, that her master may see her eat?

And would not a young lady feel far more independent, and hold up her head with a far prouder mien, if, when she goes to a theatre, she pay her half of the cab fare, of the dinner, of the tickets, and of the supper? Why should she be a pensioner for her amusements upon mere man?

And why should he pay out eleven dollars for a bunch of long-stemmed roses, or a clump of violets with a yard of purple ribbon, and send said floral offering around to her house? Who is she that she should be tricked out in bouquets like a prize horse? Would it not be more in keeping with woman's new-found live-your-own-lifeness if he were to send to her a flower catalogue, indicate with a blue pencil the kind that he would admire to see her have, and let her pay for her posies herself?

Money is the real badge of servitude. It is economic dependence, they tell us, that is throttling femininity.

Budding suffragettes, therefore, might do well to reflect that if they wish Simon-pure individuality they should insist upon Dutch treat. Then, instead of being "his girl," some one to be sheltered and fought for and paid for by him, she would be a comrade, an equal, and, possibly, a superior.

If you are going to strike at the very core and

gist of the whole matter of feminine subserviency, girls, you must pay your own way.

Otherwise you may be some day nothing but a wife.

OVER AND OVER FOREVER

THE other day I had a conversation with a genuine old troglodyte. He lived in an old town, in a large house surrounded by a cast-iron fence. There were a stone dog and a fountain in the yard.

He belonged to one of the first families. One of his ancestors had heaped up a lot of money by making patent medicine, investing in real estate and never letting go of a nickel without a cry of pain. Subsequent generations had managed to sit on the money, so that the present scions of the house are the real thing. The females start playing bridge in the morning, and the males buy polo ponies and are deeply interested in club matters.

The gentleman I talked with has nice side whiskers, is head trustee of the church and the denominational college, is past grand high hewgag in the lodge, and has a large library of books bound in morocco with his "crest" stamped thereon.

He spoke to me in this wise: "This talk of equality is all bosh. Why, children in the same family have different ability. If you would distribute the entire wealth of the country, giving each inhabitant an equal portion, within a week some would have plenty and many would have nothing. Some men are born with genius, brains, and leadership, and some are born helpless and without initiative." And so on to infinity, and nausea.

Isn't that funny? For a hundred years or so it has been reiterated that all the equality anybody is clamoring for is equality of opportunity, equality before the law, the absence of unearned privilege, and has no reference whatever to natural capacity. Never in the history of language did the equality of democracy refer to personal worth or force.

Still, I suppose, a hundred years from now old gentlemen will be sitting on front porches and pooh-poohing the idea of all men being equal.

The beauty of social and intellectual life is its inequalities. It is because some people are better, wiser, and shrewder than others that life is so interesting. The garden of human souls contains more different species than can be found amongst the flora of the earth.

And it is precisely to preserve and emphasize these natural irregularities that we want justice and a square deal.

It is the inherited irregularities of money and birth that produce intellectual and spiritual dead levels.

When all babies "start at the scratch," all have an equal opportunity to make the most of their natural abilities, we will see human diversity in its full charm.

It is not aristocracy, but artificial aristocracy; not nobility, but humbug nobility; not the real superior class, but the non-superior, privilege-maintained class, that democracy threatens.

A SUCCESSFUL WOMAN

THERE is a woman of my acquaintance who is a success. She is not rich, not gifted in the usual arts that gain notoriety, not young and peachy, not celebrated.

She is in quite moderate circumstances, and lives with her husband in a flat in a neighborhood that is not "select." She has no children.

She is past fifty, and glad of it.

Why is she successful?

Because she is cheerful, and because she cheers everybody around her.

And she is cheerful because she is the one woman out of, say, fifty I know who has succeeded in perfectly ADJUSTING herself to her surroundings.

The secret of the art of life is ADJUSTMENT, and whoever can accomplish that is entitled to be called successful. And to this title no other person has a right.

No human being is able to secure an entirely ideal environment. No woman ever lived who had a perfect husband, perfect children, a perfect home, perfect clothes, a perfect income, and perfect friends. Those who complain because they lack in any one of these respects are foolish, and know nothing of how to take hold of life.

This woman is content with the husband she has, she loves him for precisely what he is, and does not want to make him over. To have tinkered him and changed him to suit her fancy of what a husband ought to be was, of course, impossible, though many a silly woman wrecks her happiness at that task. She has done the better thing: She has ADJUSTED herself to the man as he is.

Homekeeping is her lot. So she has ADJUSTED herself to it. She has learned to love it. Her home is beautiful within, restful, tasteful, altogether delightful.

Her income is at a certain figure. To that figure she has ADJUSTED all her desires. She lives just as contentedly as if the figure were ten times as great.

She said to me the other day: "I wish you would write something to persuade women to love the common things, the everyday things. You ask me why I am so contented. It is because I love everything I see constantly about me. I love that chair, that table, that desk, those pictures, curtains, and rugs. They are all friends of mine.

"Every piece of glass or china on my table means something to me. There is not an article in this apartment that does not please me when I look at it.

"I love my friends. I love my day's duties. I love the way we live.

"When any thought of unlove presents itself to me, I put it away, just as if it were unclean. I will not give room to dislikes."

This woman is a point of sunshine in a cloudy world. If the Lord were angry with the city, as He was wroth against Sodom, and should look about to see if there were at least three souls worth while, for whose sake He might spare the town from His consuming fire, this woman would be one of the saving sort. For she is a radiating centre of helpfulness. She boosts all spirits.

Any woman can be successful, as this woman is, if she will learn the art of ADJUSTMENT. For better than a billion dollars it is to be adjusted. Better than having everything just as you'd like it, is to like things just as they come to you.

FRIED CHICKEN

WHAT are we coming to? Whither are we drifting? And oh, times and oh, manners!

The chief high worshipful of the United States Food Research Department, Mary E. Pennington, now takes the stand and deposes that FRIED CHICKEN is bad for us. That is to say, fried chicken that is fresh killed.

She withdraws her objection provided that the fowl "after being killed be kept in dry, cold air for twenty-four hours while the flesh loses its heat. Then it should be ripened from three to ten days in a temperature of 32 degrees. Then," she says, "your chicken will be fit for cooking and eating."

This, of course, is prohibitive. Few farms and families have cold-storage houses. The plan in operation since the days of Adam is to send one of the boys out into the yard to chase the devoted pullet seven times around the barn, finally to sit on it, and then wring its neck. Shortly after this the hired girl dresses it, and ere the sun sets it is on the table bringing joy and gladness to the inwards of the family.

I cannot get over the conviction that these scientific people are set upon robbing us of our most delectable things to eat. Naturally we would not strike a woman, but why does the Pennington lady attack us at the very core and citadel of our national gustatory treasure?

For, I put it to the reader as man to man, was any dish ever so downright, plum GOOD as fried chicken?

All other forms of preparing the fowl fade into drabness beside this. Roast chicken, baked chicken, smothered chicken, fricasseed chicken, stewed chicken, pressed chicken, and devilled chicken—I take my stand with regulation southern fried chicken against them, one and all.

Not jointed with the meataxe, after the manner of restaurants, but with all the joints separated carefully where the Creator made them, then rolled in flour and put into a skillet of lard and turned faithfully until a golden brown. Then pile the pieces high on the platter before dad, and have all the Browns and Robinsons to dinner, and plenty of real gravy and mashed potatoes, and I, for one, don't care what becomes of me.

I have eaten the vaunted delicacies of the Old World and of the New; I have eaten bouillabaisse at Marseilles, goulash at Vienna, paprika schnitzel at Munich, goose liver pie at Strasburg, sole at Marguery's in Paris, whitebait at Greenwich, beans in Boston, and oysters at Baltimore; but above them all FRIED CHICKEN, when turned out by the deft hands of a real Negro mammy, has, in the language of an ex-president, got them all beat to a frazzle.

All Americans should rally to repel this invasion of our most sacred institution. Alas! the Philistines are upon us. In what hotel or restaurant can you get old-fashioned fried chicken and gravy? Where in Europe can you find it? They know it not. Ask for it and the waiter looks at you as if he thought you were toying with him.

Hence to arms! If we must lose all our palladiums and historic institutions let us go down like heroes, with the banner of "FRIED CHICKEN" nailed to the mast.

LEARN THANKSGIVING FROM THE HAVE-NOTS

THE President has proclaimed the annual day of Thanksgiving. Possibly that comes to you as a joke. What have I to be thankful for? you ask, and then begin to run over the list of your grievances.

But go and see the have-nots, and maybe you will learn something, if you are not a hopeless whiner.

Visit the have-not nations. Live a while in Russia or Mexico, have your opinions suppressed, your property confiscated, your life threatened, all without justice; perhaps then you may get a few thrills when you look at the American flag.

Return, in your mind, to former ages; feel how it seems to have the nobility despise, curse, and rob you, and treat you as a dog; to have a state church clap you in prison or roast you in the public square for daring to think; to have solemn magistrates condemn your mother to be hanged as a witch; to have your daughters outraged by the lord of the manor and your sons killed fighting his battles.

If your skin is black, go back sixty years and

live among the have-nots of Liberty, and be sold in the market place as a chattel.

If you are well, turn to the have-nots of health, to the hospitals, where the crowded prisoners of pain would give the world to walk and eat and work as you now do. Go to the dim chamber of the invalid, listen to the consumptive's cough, the dyspeptic's groan, the raving of the fevered and moan of the suffering and smitten. Then, if you are anything of a man, come out and hire some one to kick you for complaining ever.

The have-nots of sound; observe the deaf and dumb, not to gloat over your advantages, but to realize what music and the voices of people and the gift of speech mean to you.

Watch the pathetic faces of the have-nots of light; and, seeing the blind, learn to be humbly grateful toward that fate that grants to you the light of heaven.

Do you know the have-nots of love? Consider them, and if one heart ever so simple loves you, be thankful. Mark the deserted wife, her dream shattered, her heart broken, her children fatherless, and the burden of care upon her shoulders; and, if you have a husband that's half decent, be thankful.

Go to the wronged, betrayed husband; look upon him; and if you have a faithful wife who believes in you and is glad because of you, be thankful.

Little girl, little boy, have you a mother that

hugs you up, and a daddy that's proud of you? Think of the have-nots, the boys and girls whose mother is still and gone or whose father is no more, and be as thankful as you can.

Have you children? Call to mind the have-nots, the mother whose loneliness is that most bitter of all, the loneliness of the empty arms, of a breast where once cuddled a curly head.

Then think of the worried, wretched, remorseful, perverted, of all those whose conscience stings them, and, if you have the comfortable self-respect of decency, be thankful.

Visit, in your mind, the wide realm of the dead and half-dead. You have the unspeakable gift of LIFE. You can walk in the sun, and breathe the sweet air, and get the message of trees, mountains, and ocean; for you the flowers blow, and the snow falls, and the hearth-fire burns, and children's voices sound, and the light of love kindles in some one's eyes.

Be thankful for life.

Think of the have-nots, and reflect. Who am I that I should not also be among them?

GEORGE WASHINGTON, GENTLEMAN

THE most significant thing about George Washington, it seems to me, that fact about him which our young folks would best note and imitate in him, is that he was a GENTLEMAN.

After all, the finest compliment we can pay any man is to say he is a gentleman. Not that he is a spurious gentleman, an idler, a spendthrift, and a dandy, but that he is a real man, and gentle.

One of the best descriptions of a gentleman is to be found in the words of St. Paul. Let me paraphrase them:

"A gentleman suffereth long, and is kind; envieth not; vaunteth not himself and is not puffed up; doth not behave himself unseemly; seeketh not his own; is not easily provoked; and thinketh no evil."

If you will analyze this list (found in I. Cor. xiii, 4, 5) you will find these eight marks of a gentleman, to wit: Patience, Humaneness, Absence of Envy, Humility, Courtesy, Unselfishness, Self-Control, and High-Mindedness. In proportion as a man has these elements, whether he be a section hand on a railway or a millionaire's son, he is a gentleman.

And whoever has the opposite traits is no gentleman, even if he wear a dress suit and have a college education, to wit: Impatience, Cruelty, Envy, Pride, Discourtesy, Selfishness, Petulance, and Suspicion.

By these tests George Washington was the Foremost Gentleman of America, and indeed far outclassed any prominent person of his time in the world.

His patience was amazing. What hero in history bore greater burdens, and with such unswerving fortitude? In the turmoil of his day all men turned to him as the one strong, rock-like figure, the embodiment of the highest quality of manhood in the New World.

He was Humane. Under his dignity was a warm heart. Not a vicious, cruel, or resentful act is in his record.

He had no Envy, which perhaps is the very meanest feeling common among mortals. Another's success pleased him. The cynic remark of La Rochefoucauld was untrue at least in him: "In the adversity of our best friends we often find something that is not exactly displeasing."

He had Humility, perhaps the greatest of virtues, as Pride is the sure sign of a petty nature. He never coveted prominence. He never struggled for office. He ruled only because it was the best way he could serve. He refused a crown, and retired gladly from the presidency.

He was Courteous. This is an acid test of

greatness. The small man's first impulse, when clothed with a "little brief authority," is to domineer. How many a false great man betrays his vulgar soul by rudeness and disregard of others' feelings!

He was Unselfish. He "sought not his own." A coarse nature is sensitive about his "rights." He is alert to his advantage. He wants all that is coming to him. But when you meet a great soul you find no trace of the pig in it. His noble disinterestedness rises upon you like the sun.

He was Self-Controlled. You find in him none of that petulance and irritation, of those storms of alternate self-pity and self-conceit you see in Napoleon. Napoleon had great talents; Washington was a great man.

He was High-Minded. He "bore all things, believed all things, hoped all things, endured all things." He trusted men. He was slow to listen to slander. He clung stubbornly to his ideals concerning his country.

He was not perhaps what the world would call a saint. He had his imperfections, his limitations. He was not a superman.

But he was a GENTLEMAN.

> And thus he bore without abuse
> The grand old name of gentleman,
> Defamed by every charlatan,
> And soiled with all ignoble use!

He was a GENTLEMAN; and you cannot go

amiss, young man, if you love that fine old face that looks down upon you from its frame on the wall, where your grandfather hung it, and if you strive to mould your life after the example of George Washington.

FREEDOM AND KNOWLEDGE FOR WOMEN

FREEDOM without knowledge is a curse.

To leave a child of six without guardianship would be criminal, because he has not knowledge enough to keep out of danger.

A lot of ignorant savages in a state of entire freedom would proceed to butcher one another.

Hence a thorough system of education is recognized as essential among people who wish to live in a democracy.

American girls are the freest in the world.

Europe is amazed at them.

Here girls come and go as they please, and have the independence of men. In Europe they are carefully guarded at home, educated in convents or in rigidly sequestered schools, their courting days are strictly chaperoned, and their marriage is managed for them.

There are not a few who decry our custom, holding that woman's liberty is too dangerous a thing, and that parents should maintain closer surveillance.

But the real trouble is not that girls have too much freedom, but that they do not have enough knowledge.

A system that keeps girls in ignorance of the most vital facts and laws of life, that makes total lack of information about their bodies and the functions thereof to be a sort of religious and moral excellence, and then turns them loose upon their own responsibility to mingle freely with men, is absurd.

The first right of a woman is not to be protected; it is to know, so that she can protect herself.

The movement for "the emancipation of woman" is good. They have as much claim to liberty as men. But it is cruel and illogical to enlarge their freedom to equal man's without at the same time doing something to equip them with that knowledge the lack of which makes freedom a road to ruin.

We cannot return to the old way of chaperonage and put high walls around women to save them. That is not in line with progress. It would be to turn again to orientalism, or medievalism. What we can and must do is to make virtue the twin sister of intelligence and not of ignorance.

The second wife of Napoleon was brought up as a child with particular seclusion; she was not allowed to see males even among the domestic animals. She was fond of frogs, but even the male frogs were exterminated. That is the sort of thing the old regime called "purity." In the minds of a great many worthy people innocence means still utter lack of knowledge.

But our mothers are as chaste as our daughters. The hospital nurse may be as chaste-minded as the young miss in an exclusive "finishing school." And the soul of a happily married man is much more likely to be "pure" than that of a celibate.

By all means loose the bonds of women and set them free; but do not imagine you can do this without peril unless at the same time you get rid of your ideas of feminine ignorance being necessary to virtue.

THE WRITTEN EXAMINATION

Not long ago a little girl of thirteen, in one of our public schools, tried to take poison because she dreaded the examination set for the next day. She was rescued by her companions.

Also a student in the University of Pennsylvania committed suicide because, as was discovered by inquiring among his fellow students, "he was of an extremely nervous temperament and was repeating his second year's work as a result of having failed to pass his examinations."

The name of the system-worshipping and marble-hearted teacher who invented examinations is happily buried in obscurity. His soul probably haunts all dark schoolhouses and frightens all little boys and girls who sit up late cramming into their noggins historical dates and geometric crazy-quilt patterns.

Written examinations are a relic of barbarism. They rank along with racks and thumbscrews, birch rods and leather straps as a method of "cruel and unusual punishment." Only these are not unusual, more's the pity!

A teacher who associates a month or so with a pupil, and at the end of that time needs a written examination to find out what the child knows, ought to resign and make place for a real teacher.

The written examination is a test of but one thing, the learner's skill in writing.

Writing is an art; it is a trick, you might say, that one has by gift of God or by practice. Because I can tell about a matter is no sign that I know much about it.

I can probably write a better essay on horse-shoeing than any blacksmith in town, because composing sentences is my trade, but if I went to shoe a horse I should very likely be kicked to death.

By going to the public library and consulting books I might prepare a paper on engineering, building bridges, or constructing office buildings that would be much more readable and interesting than any practical expert could furnish; yet who would think of hiring me to build even a hen-house?

The gift of gab and the gift of doing have nothing to do with each other.

A child might be taken by an intelligent instructor into the fields and woods daily, and learn to know intimately plant life, the habits, laws of growth, and relationship of all the flora of his neighborhood; but another child, bookish and impractical, could confine himself to his textbook in botany and give you a written examination that would rank 100 per cent., while the first child's paper would be full of haltings and confusion.

As an Exercise, as a means of practice to cultivate clearness of thought, the written examination has its place. But as a Test it is a humbug.

It is usually conducted under circumstances peculiarly trying to nervous pupils, and there are many perfectly competent minds that refuse to operate under pressure.

In boy or man let the day's work count, and let it be judged with sympathy, fairness, and appreciation.

THERE ARE OTHERS

A GOOD part of all you do is done by others.

To all your righteousness, and all your weakness and wickedness, others contribute a large share.

The criminal has some truth when he lays the blame on others. The banker might as justly place the credit for his prosperity to others.

There is a deal of humbug in individuality. Each of us is a part of our parents, neighborhood, times, of the prevalent public opinion, of soul-drifts hither and yonder. We progress or recede, we suppose; but it is like one walking in a coach while the train is going its own course with us and all our fellow-passengers.

In Bernard Shaw's "Philanderer" is a line: "If you take people seriously off the stage, why don't you take them seriously on it, where they are under some sort of decent restraint?"

Mary Lawton, an actress playing in the above-mentioned comedy, expressed an opinion, in a recent newspaper interview, that there is a deal of irony in that line which only actor people can appreciate.

"Is there any place in the world," she asks,

"where a human being is more restrained than on the stage? Any place where every result depends not only on yourself and your power, but on everything and everybody else? Is there any other profession where the crucial moment may be spoiled by a giggling schoolgirl or by a tack on the carpet? Where your entire effect is wasted if you are not given the right cue? Where your big scene may be entirely lost by a chair put in the wrong place?"

If this be the case upon the stage, then "all the world's a stage," for the like holds true everywhere.

The orator's triumph is a nicely balanced affair, of himself, his genius, and his effort on the one hand, and the time, the place, and the audience on the other. Beecher's speech in England, where he subdued the mob and won undying fame; Webster's reply to Hayne, and the addresses of Burke and John Bright make poor reading now, at least compared with their tremendous power when uttered, for the others are no longer here.

The rule holds in the smaller matters of life. Every swain knows how the success of his avowal depends fearfully upon seizing precisely the psychological moment.

There are things you can say to your wife under certain circumstances and all will be well, while if you are stupid in your choice of time and place woe be unto you!

The net effect of anything you say, for that matter, to anybody anywhere is more than half determined by the "stage setting."

The fact is, life is team play.

Most of the failures have imagined that they were the only persons on the boards.

Most of the sensitive, pouting, and soured simply missed their cue.

The best conversationalist is not the one who says the cleverest things, but the one who waits, judges, and times his remark perfectly.

Whoever will "make a hit" in this life must watch his neighbor as himself.

Much of the prominence of the prominent is due to their ability to keep off the stage while it is the turn of some one else.

It was not a bad idea of Mr. Roosevelt to visit Africa and South America.

And to all those who suffer the pangs of a neglected ego, and who for one reason or another feel that they have hardly won the applause in life they deserved, it may be well to hand the homely observation:

"There are others!"

REAL GREATNESS

JACOB H. SCHIFF, at the annual meeting of the Hebrew Free Loan Society of New York, said the other day, when he was introduced as a "great man":

"Greatness often comes from accident or favor, and if this lifts us above the multitude it should carry with it the realization of greater responsibilities on our part toward others."

And herein Mr. Schiff showed one trait at least of a great man, and said a great thing.

For you can distinguish a great from a small man in this, that when riches, or honors, or prominence come to him the great man is humbled and sobered by his sense of duty, and by his consciousness of how little after all he had to do with it.

No sincere soul really thinks he is superior. Success "comes" to us. No man earns it; or, rather, the one who earns it is denied it as often as not.

Oliver Wendell Holmes described how an idea "came" to him, striking him like a bullet, as he expressed it.

Every creative mind has felt this, how things

"just come." The composer of music, the painter, the sculptor, the novelist, dramatist and orator, the inventor, all have that sense of recipiency. Only the egotistic fool thinks he is the author of his own conceptions.

Socrates had his "daimon" that whispered to him suggestions. And every other great constructive soul has had that peculiar feeling of being played upon by some force or spirit not of himself.

Only little souls are cocky and chesty and greedy for praise, whether they deserve it or not. These are the plagiarists, copiers, and second-raters of the world.

The same is true of the greatly rich. For there are contemptible rich and noble rich.

Under existing economic conditions a man may inherit a million dollars. In proportion as he regards it as "mine, to do with as I please," he is small. He probably will spend it in luxuries and amusements. He and his set are nuisances. Their very existence is immoral.

But if he realizes that destiny, under its laws, has put this wealth upon him, for no merit of his own, and that the high and serious task of administering it for the welfare of mankind is laid on his shoulders, then he becomes great.

So also if a man makes his own fortune. He still perceives, if he be great, that "accident or favor" has played into his hands, and he can have no peace nor self-respect unless he gives himself over to doing what he can to help those less fortunate.

This is the modern conscience, which is better and sounder than the conscience of any other age.

More and more the magnificent ones of earth are hearing the dim voice of that something or somebody, call it God, call it humanity, saying to them:

"What hast thou done with the talent LENT thee?"

HAPPY DRUGS

LET us suppose there is a Devil.

I do not say there is; but suppose there is, some being, a sort of vicious god, who has a grudge against the human race, who is thoroughly malicious, and takes delight in ruining men and women, and gloats over their physical agonies, mental torments, and spiritual heart-breaks.

If there be such an Evil Spirit, he no doubt considers the HABIT-FORMING DRUG his bright particular masterpiece. For such drugs have produced more misery to the square inch in humanity than any other agency.

In every human being there is implanted the desire for happiness. We all want to "feel good." The normal means for producing the sensation of contentment consists in obeying the laws of hygiene and of morals.

Whoever conforms to the rule of nature as to his body, and of God as to his mind, has inward success; that is, he is cheerful, sound, and strong.

And now comes the Devil and says:

"You want to feel good? Why follow the poky road to health? That takes self-control and will-power. It is hard. I will show you the easiest way. Just swallow this HAPPY DRUG."

The Happy Drugs have been known from time immemorial. The oldest is Alcohol. It has got itself woven into the customs and the imagination of the people until many cannot conceive of having a good time without it. It is the expected thing at weddings, wakes, and all manner of celebrations. In vain Intelligence has shown that it is a poison, habit-forming, weakens the heart and hardens the arteries. "What the hell do we care?"

A man requested permission the other day to visit the Tombs prison in New York. Upon searching him the officer found some envelopes containing the drug heroin. In these envelopes were notes addressed to various inmates. One of them read:

"Dear Mac—A little Happy Dust. Regards to Jim and all the boys."

Heroin, a drug allied to morphine, but deadlier and cheaper than either that or cocaine, is the latest dope of the slums, the latest invention of the able and efficient Mr. Devil.

Dr. Jackson R. Campbell, who has been prison physician for some years, says: "Heroin is one of the most desperate dangers that confront our race. The stuff is so cheap—10 cents' worth of it is enough to produce the 'sensation' for two or three hours—that any boy or girl can afford to buy it. But, once accustomed to it, the user needs more and more, and will commit any crime to get it.

"Within a mile's radius of 149th street and Third avenue, the Bronx," the doctor declared, "there are at least a thousand victims of the heroin habit, including many boys and girls. Police records show many arrests of children for having the stuff."

There may be people who do not believe in Hell, but they are not found among the Happy Drug users. THEY KNOW THERE IS A HELL. THEY LIVE IN IT.

Let any boy or girl—or grown person, for that matter—who reads this THINK a minute! THE DRUG THAT MAKES YOU HAPPY IS THE MOST LYING, CHEATING, CRUEL, AND TERRIBLE ENEMY YOU HAVE IN THE WORLD. DON'T TAKE IT!

THE UNFROCKED

THERE was a curious banquet held at Paris not long ago. There met a hundred and fifty ex-priests and ex-preachers, who did not blush either for their past or for their present.

To one class of men society seems peculiarly unjust—to the "unfrocked." The man who leaves the ministry, no matter how conscientious and sincere his motives, is always looked upon askance. We persist in regarding him as if he were tainted with the flavor of desertion and disloyalty.

Why? Is it not more honorable to leave holy orders, when one no longer believes the articles of faith, or when one is convinced of the inutility of the institution, when the development of one's mind and heart has led him honestly to these convictions, than to remain and be insincere?

Does not the church itself believe that an honest layman, no matter what his views, is better than a dishonest clergyman?

For all that, the rupture between the parson and his organization is always painful. Laymen hardly welcome him. By a strange illogicality we are usually cold to the men who enter our ranks for conscience' sake. We mistrust them; we put pressure upon them to conceal their past as something of which to be ashamed; as a rule, they have a hard time making a living.

Among the ex-clergymen at the banquet mentioned we may note three lawyers, two police magistrates, two farmers, a physician, two artists, two capitalists, one mayor, besides commercial travellers, university professors, accountants, and public school teachers.

They have formed a union which proposes, according to its by-laws, never to proselyte or in any way attempt to induce men to leave the ministry, but to extend a helping hand to those who, on their own initiative, have severed their ecclesiastical ties, and to help them in their endeavors to gain an honest livelihood.

It will do no harm to the church—it can only do good—to make the way as easy as possible for those who have ceased to be in harmony with its faith or its methods to get out.

In most instances men enter the ministry when young. When they arrive at maturity their convictions may in all honor have undergone a change. It should not be taken as a matter of course that their reluctance to continue in the ministry means a loss of religion or of personal integrity. The minister may discover that, while his religious sentiment is as profound as ever, he is not adapted by nature or gifts to be a clergyman.

His retirement from church office may be as heroic and worthy of praise as his entrance into it.

MEANING OF THE WOMAN MOVEMENT

VERY few of those engaged in the movements of modern feminism, or of those opposed, realize the depth, the tidal resistlessness, the cosmic character, of the force which is, now quietly and now with turbulence, bringing women into even higher prominence in our civilization.

Most of the things advanced women are striving for are straws, but they show the way the wind blows. Getting the vote, in itself, means little; so also mean little the wearing of trousers, the entrance into the professions or into business, or the capture of any of the superficial privileges traditionally enjoyed by men only. But as indications of the gradual feminization of the race these things mean much.

In a state of nature and of freedom, where society is not continually prevented from normal growth by wars and threatening wars, as has been the case up to this age and everywhere but in America, woman would be naturally the superior and dominant sex.

Ruskin points out that Shakespeare, and Scott, and Dante, and all the greatest masters of literature have not been mistaken in making the heroine always the stronger spiritually. It is she who is queen and disposer, it is for her the hero fights and labors, his reward and his incentive are in her keeping.

Man is the weaker vessel. Only in imperfectly developed races is the strong man master. As culture and intellectual growth advance the reins of control pass into the woman's hands.

Biologists are now intimating that it is probable that Eve was made first and that Adam is the after product created to assist in the perpetuation of the race.

That women now "look up" to men, and are usually clinging vines and leaning, dependent creatures, idle dolls or indolent playthings, is simply due to the lingering influence of centuries of artificial conditions caused by the universal presence of war.

In time to come the woman and not the man will be the Head of the Family. Hers are the children more than his; she carries them while they are being formed; her body and soul is poured into them.

In marriage the man will take the woman's name. All that he achieves will be frankly recognized as caused by her direction. Property rights will be vested in her, not in him.

She it is that has the divine beauty of face and form, and when the struggle shall have been transferred from fists and clubs to ideas and spirit potencies she will naturally assume leadership.

The farther we evolve from beasthood the nearer we approach to a woman-ruled world.

In all the things that tend to the health and soundness of mankind, and hence to "the outpopulating power" of a nation, woman is superior. She has by nature the strength that lies in chastity, loyalty, and the appreciation of the higher spiritual quantities of reverence, self-control and idealism. Man is carnal, drunken, and earthy, only kept up to the mark by the enchantment woman casts upon him.

The "mastery" of such men as Napoleon and Bismarck is crude, cheap stuff. The world to-day, and even more to-morrow, needs and will need another kind of mastery, not that of battle might, of Tammany power, of the brutal efficiency of enormous capital, but the mastery of conscience, of the sense of justice, and of the just estimate of human values.

Here woman is supreme. Hail to her, queen of the coming race!

Even to-day a man does no work worth while except it be to lay it at the feet of the woman he serves.

THEORY AND PRACTICE IN BRINGING UP CHILDREN

THE trouble with most of the theories of child-training is that the child is supposed to be located in the middle of a forty acre lot, and to be attended by three all-wise angels, who work in shifts of eight hours each and who unerringly know always just what is the matter and precisely what to do.

If there is anything more impractical and more maddening to a poor mortal parent or teacher than a grand educational programme I do not know what it is.

Several factors are invariably left out. In the first place, there are relatives. You may determine to refrain from carrying, rocking, or jiggling the baby, and to accustom him to lying in his crib without attention, but what are you going to do when Aunt Jane, who has money, comes along and insists on picking him up and showing him the boofle flowers?

You may endeavor to break him of crying and attempt to let him whine himself to sleep; but grandma has something to say about that.

And what happens to the most rational systems

of child management when the mother has four little ones cooped up in a city flat, and must take care of them and keep them from poisoning or maiming themselves, and must do this in such intervals of time as she can snatch between washing dishes, getting dinner, cleaning house, sewing, and mending?

Besides, a perfectly good mother may not be physically strong. Four vigorous little personalities demanding instant care all day may reduce her to the borders of nervous prostration. And where are the grand laws of patience and prevention when your back hurts like the toothache and you are so tired you don't know your name?

Also, a good mother may not be endowed with mental perspicacity and deep wisdom. A thousand times she does not know what to do. She may have real love and a high purpose, and do the wrong thing from sheer bewilderment or ignorance.

As for the schoolteacher, her ideal systems for developing the growing mind are usually crushed to death by numbers. Sixty children in a crowded room are too much for any human teacher. By and by she is forced to drop back into mere routine because it is impossible to give each child due care and be alive at the end of the week.

Yet, somehow, children do grow up and flourish. Weak and incompetent mothers bring up capable children, who love her and give her credit in maturer years for the best that is in them. Out of the homes of the poor come great men and noble women. Out of the overcrowded schoolroom garden human plants rise strong and fruitful.

It is because human nature is better than any scheme for bettering it; because honest love is better than shrewd handling; because motherhood is more efficacious in its instincts than any experts are in their pedagogy and psychology; and because the child absorbs helpful forces from the atmosphere of a school that far outbalance the personal guidance he misses.

UNNOTED HEROISM

THE world is full of unnoted heroism.

That is the best kind. Spectacular heroism is always a little tainted.

The man who stops a runaway horse in the city street, or the man who dives and rescues a drowning woman, or the soldier who dashes forward in the face of death, does well; but there is a better type.

Many can act nobly under the spur of sudden impulse and with an inspiring audience; but to live upon the high plane of self-sacrifice daily takes finer fibre.

There is the workman who brings home his entire week's pay every Saturday night, that it may be used for the care of wife and children, and that the balance be put in the savings bank. Some look on him as tame and dull, a routiner with no spirit; but he would like to go to the ball game as well as any man, to take his beer in the saloon and crack jokes with the boys, and to buy for himself the expensive luxuries men enjoy. He daily subdues himself in little things; heroism with him is a rule and not an exception; it is of the kind the world passes by, often misjudges and despises.

And how many women, unknown and unpraised, are living days of constant devotion to high purpose! They are hidden in homes, they are persecuted by petty economies, they have given up tastes soul-deep and renounced ambitions dear as life, just to be faithful and loyal in the small corner where destiny has placed them.

What a wonderful, divine thing is a human being! Capable of how serene heights of greatness!

Whoever would see this, however, must himself be great, for to small souls all men are worms and spiders.

And against what odds the common man maintains his character! Sensational newspapers pour into his consciousness their daily gathering of perversion, violence, and greed; novels exploit their stories of the idle and privileged class, and the morbidities of passion; almost every cult and ism exclaims against the innate evil of men and women; yet he clings to his reverences, does his work and keeps clean.

The most admirable nobility is that of the common run of people. The mass of men is better than any class of men.

You can bribe, debauch, and ruin this or that group; you cannot corrupt a whole people.

It is mankind that is steadily, persistently good. It is humanity that rejects all poisons. It is the human race that best reflects the faces of the gods.

If any one would drink of the unfailing spring of optimism, feed on the treasures of hope, learn the secret of wholesome faith, and find that sweet, strong quality in spirit that corresponds to the sanity and peace found in nature, let him study to know and to love the common people, for theirs are the infinite resources, the rich supplies, of unnoted heroism.

HOUSEWORK

THERE is no better business, no nobler nor more helpful to mankind, than housework.

And it is one of the curious quirks of the times that while we rank "home" alongside of "heaven," call it the sacredest word in the language and all that, we set housework or home-keeping down as one of the least desirable of occupations.

Nine girls out of ten would rather do anything than cook, make beds, and wash dishes.

Country girls swarm to the cities, and city girls flock to offices, to type and keep books and mind cash; leaving only those who cannot do anything else to attend to homes.

The servant girls are in the rearward of the march of labor. They have few or no organizations, no standardized training, no social standing, no rights any one is bound to respect, and no independent spirit to demand those rights.

Things also are getting worse. The disgusting custom of tipping is on the increase, insulting to the worker and demoralizing to the giver. For the tip is never anything else than a cheap and nasty substitute for paying decent wages.

The housemaid is one of the few laborers who wear distinctive uniforms, emphasizing class distinction.

The home seems to be a little corner where the snows of aristocratic sentiment linger in the spring of democracy. "Housework," says Ida Tarbell, "is the only field of labor in which there seems to be a general tendency to abandon the democratic notion and return frankly to the aristocratic regime."

And that is exactly what is the matter with domestic service. For wherever the vain, vulgar, hoity-toity idea prevails that one class of workers is inferior to another, wherever the segregative, exclusive feeling of artificial aristocracy is found, there is the soiling touch, the dirty fingers of injustice, the poison of caste.

What housework needs is the redeeming breath of democracy. There is no reason why making good biscuit and maintaining a home in order and beauty should not be as dignified a business as laying brick or attending to the plumbing. Why should not the kitchen girls have their union, their regular hours of service, and their well-defined rights, as well as the bricklayer and the plumber?

There is no department of labor where brains are more needed than in housework. The intelligent, deft, and capable maid-of-all-work can produce quite as much human contentment, joy, and gladness as any of the world's workers.

Those women who burn with the desire to do something to emancipate their sex, to make woman's lot more tolerable and light, are invited to turn their attention to improving the condition of serving girls, who need far more sympathy and get far less than shop girls.

FEAR KILLS TALK

THE joy of talk is to say what you please.

Any restraint upon the free expression of whatever pops into your mind kills conversation.

Conversation becomes a bore when people are saying what they are supposed to say. Then it is no more the free mingling of souls, for each is posing. It is dress parade.

I would rather hear a man swear than to be entertained by some one who is working at me from a sense of duty.

When you have to be careful what you say, the only refuge is silence.

Hence parsons, college presidents, and all those in high office, who are likely to be quoted, and whose chance words may upset that terrible creature known as the "young person," must take one of two alternatives; either they must speak rarely and be mindful to say nothing when they do speak, or they must practice the handling of bromidions and avoid saying anything that is fresh or has sharp corners.

New-minted speech is only for the irresponsible. Slang words especially, being the babes of language, such words as will not for years be permitted to associate with their elders, are to be used by people of no standing.

The conversation of children, when they are by themselves, or among such grown persons as put them under no bond of fear, is the most interesting of all talk. They say things that are immensely funny, that are stuffed with ingenuous feeling and piquant with rare philosophy; and for but one reason, that they do not care.

It is fear that blights talk, as it nips in the bud all flowers of the soul.

Let us stretch our legs under the table, and until long after midnight crack our jokes, tell our pet hates and loves, expose our doubts, air our heresies, give wing to our fancies, gossip freely of the neighbors, and preen our comfortable vanities, and so will our souls empty themselves and become clean vessels, holding over till to-morrow no stagnant opinions to breed spiritual malaria.

I once peddled maps, when young, and learned a speech by rote, which I repeated to every victim. By and by I came to loathe it. Also it became deliciously absurd. Which is a reasonable contradiction.

And I never go to a reception, or tea, or other regulated talkfest, and listen to the usualities bandied back and forth with well-tempered laughter, but I think of that map-peddling rigmarole, and wonder why the whole company does not break out into Gargantuan laughter at itself.

The better way for us would be to hold no

speech at all with them from whom we expect fear or favor, only make signs, and reserve our frank openings of heart for those whom we owe nothing, for those who take our chatter for amusement only.

For the rest, let us read books, or newspapers, or attend lectures. Why talk when we are afraid?

LINCOLN, DEMOCRAT, SERVANT OF ALL

It is rather unfortunate, in the interests of clear thinking, that the two leading political parties of the United States take the titles of Democrat and Republican. It makes it difficult to speak of democracy or republicanism without leading some of your auditors to fancy that you mean one of the two great job-hunting organizations.

When I call Lincoln a democrat I have, of course, no intention of identifying him with any political faction, but refer to the fact that he believed in the rule of the people and not of the classes, which is the root-meaning of democracy.

To me Lincoln was the greatest democrat that ever lived—that is, no one seems to have had such an utter confidence in the common people as he.

In the first place, he knew the people. He did not come down from some higher social level to "do them good." He was not a missionary to the people. He was one of them. He was born right. His parents, relatives, and all the neighbors of his early life were "just folks."

It was a free, wide country he lived in. Everybody worked. There were no endowed loafers, no self-styled superior class. A man was a man for a' that in Sangamon County, Illinois, in the forties and fifties. The only way to know a people is to be born of them and to have your youth soaked in their environment.

And Lincoln "sensed" the people, knew what they wanted, loved, feared, and hoped better than any other man of his age, and, possibly, of any age. He was the people's nerve, part and parcel of their body; he FELT them.

Then he esteemed them. He thought the whole people had more sense than any leader or wise statesman. You are never a genuine democrat until you think that. He expressed it in his wondrous way when he said: "You can fool some of the people all the time, and all of the people some of the time, but you can't fool all of the people all the time."

And the people, he believed, were not only wiser, but they were also honester, purer, holier, and more nearly right than any small number or specially trained or bred group. To him the will of that great people from whom he sprang was the will of God. Their grim purpose was the purpose of God. The majesty of their deep feeling he revered as if it were the majesty of God.

There was none of the clap-trap and hypocrisy of the office seeker in his appreciation of the people. It was through and through his soul.

He was not a ruler, as Julius Cæsar. He was

not a leader, nor teacher, nor guide to the people, as other great men have been. He was one of the greatest SERVANTS of the people that ever lived.

He did not "want to help" them; he knew they could help themselves if they could find the right kind of servant, and that he strove to be.

He knew the people did not need any king or general or statesman to instruct them what to do, nor any philanthropist nor billionaire to do things for them; all they wanted was to be given a chance to do things for themselves, to struggle out of their poverty by their own efforts, to remedy their own wrongs and to carry out their own reforms when they got ready.

And what Lincoln stood for is the thing America, and all the world, for that matter, needs to-day—to wit, that the people do not need so much new laws, new and fantastic schemes of government, new gospels, wise guides, benefactors, and helpers, but they simply need agents who will carry out their will; they need simple justice, a square deal, and a chance to paddle their own canoe.

The world to-day needs the faithful servant, not the superior ruler.

In Lincoln was fulfilled the words of One who also took upon Himself the form of a servant:

"And whosoever will be great among you shall be the servant of all."

A $5,000 FLEA

I SEE by the papers that Alfred Charles de Rothschild of London is said, on the authority of Edmond Perrier of the French Institute, to have paid $5,000 for a specimen of a rare variety of flea—one of the kind which is occasionally found in the skin of the sea otter. The flea is to be added to Mr. de Rothschild's entomological collection.

The other day two postage stamps were sold in Paris for $1,000. They had been issued by some island country. Immediately afterward an earthquake swallowed up the place, and only these two of the whole issue of stamps happened to escape in the mail.

Every once in a while we hear of a millionaire dropping off and leaving a large heap of junk. They shall all be eclipsed when I shy my hat into the ring.

For when my ship comes in, or when my rich uncle (joke) passes and saddles forty million plunks upon me, I know what I will do.

At present I am living quite comfortably, with one wife, plenty of bread and cheese, and with pie upon occasion; but that sort of thing will be all over.

I shall eat gamy things and drink bubbly things, and accumulate indigestion, arteriosclerosis, and headaches. Let the workingmen have vulgar health. Me for the purple pangs of plutocracy—what?

But first of all I shall buy me a flea. I must have a flea, and a bigger and fiercer one than Rothschild's. I think I shall go in for hippopotamus fleas.

Then I shall get me a couple of stamps. I shall visit the Ahkoond of Swat or Mr. Villa of Mexico and have printed a special edition of two heathen stamps, just for me, for which I shall pay $20,000 apiece, and turn all philatelists greener and purpler with envy than my stamps.

Then I shall hire a man to go up and down Europe and explore all the ragbags of royalty, and buy up the debts of all the bankrupt dukes, and ship me home nine carloads of Old Masters, eight tons of Louis Quinze and Pre-Raphaelite and European Elbert Hubbard furniture, seventy-seven wagon-loads of china and glassware, thirty bales of moth-eaten tapestry, six cords of canes, sixteen hogsheads of old armor, swords, and blunderbusses, a hundred gallons of ancient coins with green on them (specially manufactured in Florence and Rome), besides a collection of collars and cuffs, boots and buttons, napkin rings, crowns, and sceptres from the various kings, queens, and knaves of the Old World.

I will have an office into which you can enter

only by passing four rooms and five secretaries, and never allow any one at all to come and see me; and I shall live in a house in the middle of a hundred-acre woods-pasture, with two men at the gate with shotguns.

It sure will be nice to be rich. When I get lonesome I will go and play with my flea.

SHALL SHE TELL HIM?

A MOST interesting letter comes to me from a reader. She writes:

"I am nearly thirty. Some years ago I forgot, for a brief time, that I was a woman, and being unhappy, restless, and extremely foolish, I lowered myself to sin. I did not fall utterly, but in my indiscretion I stained my soul.

"After a short period my conscience awakened. I saw where I was going, and I stopped. I repented bitterly of my acts and thoughts. I asked forgiveness of Heaven, and thought that it had been granted.

"I did not think when I committed those sins that love would ever come to accuse me. But to-day I love a man, and he loves me with all his heart. He believes me to be all that a woman should be. If I tell him the facts of my past life I know he will hate me.

"Yet I feel that I do not deserve his love, and that I ought not to marry him and deceive him, as I would deceive him if I remain silent.

"What shall I do? Shall I tell him?

"I had thought repentance and right living would wipe out any sin, however great, but I can find no peace since love has come, and I stand accused before it.

"Do I deserve love? Or must I give him up, and put love away from me forever because of those early mistakes of mine?

"I know, and he has not tried to conceal it from me, that his life has not been blameless. But somehow it seems different in a woman.

"Shall I tell him?"

The "unpardonable sin" nonsense has done no end of hurt. It is not wrongdoing that permanently soils; it is continuance in it, and the persistent love of it. If you are honestly sorry that you did wrong, and not merely fearful that you will be found out, and if you have ceased evil-doing, you have a moral right to respect yourself.

The "bird with a broken wing" theory is immoral. We have all sinned, the Good Book tells us; and, for that matter, we do not need to be told; we know it. And it is the very essence of any right living to be able, by repentance and reformation, to take up life afresh, "with a conscience void of offense toward God and man."

As for your husband, or husband to be, he is not your confessor. You are your own judge as to your fitness for wifehood. You know whether you come to him worthily or not. And if he is not satisfied to take you as you are, and upon your own estimate of yourself, you would better let him go.

Hold on to common sense. Be just to yourself, or you cannot be just to others. It is very easy to fall into the luxury of self-condemnation, to wallow in remorse; but a diseased, morbid, and unintelligent conscience can do quite as much harm as no conscience at all.

Keep your chin up. Tell the truth in preference to a lie, but remember there are times when our highest duty is to keep our mouth shut.

To believe that you are forever ruined and hopeless is about the worst belief you can indulge in. And rest assured if you are now sure in your own heart that you have put away forever the follies of the past, love can and will come and keep you sound and clean in the future.

Old as human sin is human and divine forgiveness, and old as the blackness of weakness and perversion is the whiteness of the new life built upon the death of the old. Says Whittier:

> For still the new transcends the old
> In signs and tokens manifold;
> Slaves rise up men; the olive waves,
> With roots deep set in battle graves.

THE UNDYING CREDULITIES

"SUPERSTITION," says Lippert, "has a tenacity of life which no religion possesses."

In the second part of his "Christentum, Volksglaube und Volksbrauch" there is an interesting list of pre-Christian superstitions still prevalent in Europe.

Almost all of our Christmas customs are survivals of heathendom, though made beautiful by the spirit of the Christ-Child.

The religious feeling is the property of certain minds, of a limited number, even among church folk; but superstitions are in every mind. Some people are religious; all people are superstitious.

They have changed religions several times in England; they still retain the old Druid fancies. Long after old faiths lose their power old credulities hold their grip. When the gods fled from Greece they settled in the backwoods of Christendom. They ceased to be respectable and adored; they became bush-whackers and feared.

The Venus that inspired Praxiteles became the Venus that lived in the mountain and lured Tannhäuser to his ruin.

The religions of India are dead; the folk-lore of India is still alive.

What is preached in temples varies with time; what is told to children by mothers at bedtime is fixed and eternal.

The theses of theologians in one century are obsolete in the next century; but Little Red Ridinghood and Jack the Giant Killer are as fresh with youth and interest now in the nursery as they ever were.

Bluebeard will outlive Napoleon; and the Old Woman that Lived in a Shoe has a dynasty of fame beyond that of Queen Victoria.

When beliefs disappear from the consciousness of the race they sink into the subconsciousness. The visible river of faith becomes subterranean streams of credulity.

The high priests that ruled Egypt are no more; the prophets of Israel have ceased; the medieval monks and hermits have gone; the echoes of Luther and Loyola, Calvin, John Knox, and Wesley grow fainter; new preachers, new gospels, new moral programmes appear; but the clairvoyants, palmists, fortune-tellers, astrologers, table-rappers, and all the tribe of hocus-pocus are doing as lively a business, and by the same methods, in New York, London, and Paris as they ever did in Samarcand and Heliopolis, Palmyra, and Babylon.

Religion is progressive development and adapts itself to the development of the intellect. Superstition is the immovable orthodoxy, that adapts itself to nothing, reigning forever in its pristine shapes.

They that play at the Stock Exchange and the horse-race and the poker game are too advanced to go to church; but they believe in luck, wear charms, and are afraid of Friday the thirteenth, precisely as the men of Nineveh. They are the truly orthodox.

THE UNBELIEVER

"As sure as the sun rises," said the Believer.

"That," replied the Unbeliever, "is not sure at all."

Believer—What do you mean? Would you dispute the sun?

Unbeliever—Certainly! Why not? The sunrise is only one of those things everybody takes for granted. You have perhaps seen it a half dozen times. From that you reason that it takes place every day. But I doubt if the sun rises when there is no one present to see it. Would a theatrical company go on with a performance if every seat in the house were empty?

Believer—You are crazy.

Unbeliever—Rational, you mean. The probability is that this sunrise business is just another scheme of hotel proprietors of mountain resorts, of farmers who want their farmhands to get up early, and of other interested people. Whenever you find a permanent institution which imposes upon the whole of mankind you will find graft behind it.

Believer—What a charming belief!

Unbeliever—Don't accuse me of belief! I hate

the word. I have only unbelief. That alone is consistent with high mentality. It is the dupes of the world who believe. It is the sharpers of the world who live upon beliefs.

Believer—Yes?

Unbeliever—Sure! If there were no confidence there could be no confidence men. If there were no trust there could be no heartbreaks. If there were no assurance there could be no disappointment.

Believer—But, man, you know the sun rises every day, and will rise to-morrow.

Unbeliever—Nothing of the kind! When I see it rise, I know it rises. When I don't see it, I do not know. I refuse to take other people's word. And how do you know the sun will come up to-morrow? Simply because you saw it to-day and yesterday. But because a thing has happened twice or three times or a million times, is that any proof it will go on happening? I took Christabel out to dinner last night and the night before; do I have to go on taking her out to dinner forever?

Believer—Good! You have convinced me. I shall begin by doubting the things that make me unhappy. First, I shall doubt the cocksureness of my own reason. That will land me in a comfortable confidence in my instincts. Then I shall register a doubt against that fixed belief of yours in the evil of all men and the cussedness of things in general. By that I shall bounce back again into my old faith in good men and my trust that all things work out for the best. I shall doubt the frailty of women and so come again to my belief in virtue. I shall doubt doubt, and hence have faith in faith.

Unbeliever—But——

Believer—But me no buts! If I am to be a doubter I am going the whole hog.

Unbeliever—Amazing!

Believer—Not at all. Rational! Superrational!

WHEN THE WORLD WOKE UP

JOHN FISKE calls the thirteenth century "the glorious century." In H. L. Chamberlain's recent volume is a list of some of the wonders of that time. I condense them here, to give the reader a bird's-eye view of that century, in which the world woke up.

In Europe the Hansa and Rhenish Alliance of Cities was formed, "paving the way," says Ranke, "for civic liberty and the formation of powerful states."

The Magna Charta was proclaimed in England in 1215, "a solemn proclamation of the inviolability of the great principle of personal freedom and personal security."

During this century the slave trade disappeared from European countries (except Spain).

Money begins to take the place of barter in buying and selling; the foundation of modern business is laid.

Paper is first manufactured, "the most momentous industrial achievement till the invention of the locomotive."

The religious awakening under Francis of Assisi occurred. Thode says: "This movement gives men the first forewarning of universal freedom of thought."

Scholars like Albertus Magnus and Roger Bacon prepared the ground for modern natural science by turning the attention of men from logical disputes to mathematics, physics, astronomy, and chemistry.

"A new era in mathematical science began," says Cantor; this was especially the work of Leonardo of Pisa, who was the first to introduce to Europe the Indian (falsely called Arabian) numerical signs; also Jordanus Saxo, who initiated us into the art of algebraic calculation (also originally invented by the Hindoos).

The first dissection of a human body took place at the close of this century.

Dante lived in the thirteenth century.

Adam de la Halle, born in 1240, was the first master of note in the treatment of counterpoint, so that with him modern music in a strict sense begins. Gevaert, the musical authority, writes: "Henceforward we must consider the thirteenth century, formerly so despised, as the beginner of all modern art."

Giotto, Cimabue, and Niccolo Pisano were of the thirteenth century; and to them the world is indebted for a perfectly new art, that of modern painting.

Almost all the masterpieces of Gothic architecture, "the incomparable beauty of which we to-day admire, but cannot imitate," originated in this century.

The first purely secular university, Bologna, was founded shortly before 1200.

In the thirteenth century Marco Polo made his expeditions of discovery which laid the foundations of our knowledge of the earth's surface. This beginning of world geography is the germ that ripens into world-civilization and world-government, which we are now commencing to grasp as an ideal.

But, most significant of all, it was in the thirteenth century that the long and horrid darkness that had closed upon men's minds began to lift.

The western world ceased to sleep and to dream and began to awaken, to live, to do.

"Men, so to speak, turned a corner in their course, the past vanished from their sight, henceforth they belong to the future."

The declaration of the Magna Charta sounds as a trumpet blast for all modern morals, a sentiment not yet realized, but understood and toward which we aim:

"No one may be condemned except in accordance with the laws of the land. Right and justice may not be bought nor refused."

Since June 15, 1215, when this decree went forth, it has become a law above all laws; senates and kings must bow to it.

THE UNKNOWN FUTURE

A GIRL went to a physician, who felt of her pulse, peeked into her eye, listened to her heart action, and announced that she had no more than six years to live.

At least, so it is presented in a recent Parisian play, and one critic proposed the query: "If you suddenly learned that you would die in six years, what would you do, and how would you pass the remainder of your allotted time?"

We cannot think of this without depression. And this leads us to realize that one of the chief ingredients in the sum of our contentment is our ignorance of the future.

The only reason why fortune tellers may be tolerated, together with gypsy seers, dealers in premonitions, and forewarners, is that they lie. If they tell the truth occasionally it is by accident.

The one thing we can never know, the eternally inscrutable region, is the future.

A European astronomer, Jean Mascart, feels confident he can tell what the weather is going to be a month in advance. The old-fashioned almanac claimed even more, for it foretold droughts and cold spells for the whole year. John Stuart Mill expressed the opinion that a science of the future might be created, indicating coming events by well known laws.

But so far all efforts to peer ahead are not in anywise to be depended on. For which let us be thankful!

What a calamity it would be if science should not only register the weather of next July, but the various happenings which are to come to us in the course of our existence, the disease which finally is to take us off, and even the date of our death!

Imagine a poor wretch who from childhood should know exactly the experiences he is to go through, and should thus play his part in the drama of life carefully following an unescapable programme!

No more surprises, and they are the chief pleasures of life.

No more mystery, and that is life's beauty.

No more fancy and wonder about to-morrow, and thus to-day would be asphyxiated.

No more liberty, no more spirit of adventure, no gay meeting of the dawn with expectant heart.

You couldn't even commit suicide, unless it were in the programme.

No more courting and the delicious uncertainty as to her answer; you would know that you would get her anyhow, or not; why flutter?

The great tragedy, or comedy, of life is often

disappointing in the end, but at least it is mighty interesting as we go along, thanks to the blessed curtain that

> hides from us all the book of fate,
> All but the page prescribed, the present date.

If the scientist should offer us a knowledge of the future we should tell him to go hang. Life is poky enough as it is; at least leave us those graces of surprise, of mystery, and of adventure without which existence would be a bore twice cursed.

THE NEW NOBILITY

THERE will always be a nobility and a commons. Democracy does not operate to level all people to one grade. It creates distinctions as sharp as those of the old world systems. There will be as great a difference between a noble and a vulgar person under democracy as there is between a duke and a stable boy in the artificial class scheme of England. There will be more; for often in European society the real character of the stable boy is not far removed from that of the duke.

In the real gradations of nobility rank is of no significance. A lady who is a leader in the smart set may be low and common, and the lady who runs the typewriter may be high and gentle.

As a rule, extreme wealth which creates idleness produces vulgarity, causing narrowness, pride, and selfishness; and extreme poverty has the same effect, as it stunts, imbrutes and clogs life. Beyond this, one's circumstances mean little or nothing in cultural value.

Real nobility may be known by these marks:

A certain fine cleanliness of mind. An ignoring and an unconsciousness of the body and its appetites. Moderation in eating and drinking. Perfect control over the sex instinct. The body must be got out of the way, else one always gives an impression of grossness that is offensive.

Genuine humility of spirit. Not servility, but a noble indifference to praise and honors. To want high office, to want to be noticed, admired, and envied, is to be, to a degree, coarse natured.

To push one's self, to advertise, to scheme for prominence, may be good business, but it is not noble. This does not apply to the advertisement of one's goods which he has for sale, but to one's self.

All vanity, boasting, talking of self and of one's own achievements or money, a loud tone of voice, the habit of breaking in upon the conversation of others, too much prominence of the pronoun I, these are low.

The real nobility never dress strikingly. The woman who wears a garment that attracts attention because of its startlingness shows a streak of commonness. The height of good dressing is to be unobserved, said Beau Brummel.

A fondness for jewelry and perfumes is a mark of a lack of refinement.

Real nobleness is indicated by a taste for simplicity, a quietness in speech, in manner, in one's furniture and house. All display, whether in a Fifth avenue mansion or a Bowery necktie, is coarse.

Luxury is an unfailing mark of a low nature,

particularly when it is accompanied by extravagance and debts.

The noble mind respects itself, and will not be imposed upon. It is unafraid, but not bullying.

Nobleness is shown by courtesy, by an unfailing regard for the feelings of others, by an inborn gentleness and modesty; just as coarseness of nature is shown by the opposite kind of thing.

Testing yourself and others by these standards, you will be surprised at the number of genuinely noble people you know. You find them everywhere; one may be selling newspapers at the street corner, one may work in your kitchen, one may be a millionaire, one a poor man.

The most striking presentation I have ever seen of the kind of an aristocrat democracy stands for is in Forbes-Robertson's "Passing of the Third Floor Back."

WORD PICTURES

TRY to realize words, especially the strong, vital words.

One way to do this is to create by your imagination a picture that shall express the word. Make your own cinematograph show. Learn how to entertain yourself a little by your own fancy and you will not be so helpless—dependent upon other people and outside things for amusement.

Here are some hints. Start from them and create your own scenes.

STRENGTH. A strong man ploughing. His face is ruddy, smiling, vigorous. His hair is crisp, his eyes blue and clear. Sleeves uprolled and collar downturned display his healthy skin. He is pausing for a moment's rest, his hand upon the plough. His two huge Norman horses stand, deep breathing, ready, docile. Watch that man work.

POWER. You stand at a little way station in the country. The lightning express goes by. You hear its owl-like hoot in the distance, see its headlight miles away as a dim star; it approaches, whirls past with crash and shriek as of a thousand giants. There is a blur of light, there are streams of sparks, a whirlwind of smoke, and it is gone; soon you hear its owl-hoot again in the distance. Power!

DOMINION. A big, helpful word, to get one's soul out of the swamps of pettiness. See Gibraltar, huge, impregnable, cannon-pierced, dominating all about.

PEACE. A summer lake. Sheep asleep in a meadow. Motionless trees. A soft half-moon silvering all with a veil of mystery. A house, dark, with drawn blinds.

WISDOM. Recall Michael Angelo's "Moses." Let this statute rise before you, massive, majestical. Wonder what those lips might say if, as the artist once commanded, it should "speak."

HOPE. Dawn. A rising sun, just peeping above the hill. Apple blossoms budding. Fuzzy little chickens running about. The red cock crowing. A young girl dressed in white standing at the open door of a cottage, her eyes smiling.

And jocund day
Stands tiptoe on the misty mountain tops.

FAITH. A long wedge-line of wild geese flying northward on a spring night. You hear their honk-honk dropping from the vague dimness above. A sailing boat drawing toward port, yet out of sight of land; a pilot with his eye on the compass and his hand upon the wheel. A farmer planting seed, covering them up, and going away.

Strength, power, dominion, peace, wisdom, hope, faith.

Let us get the habit of thinking these things, of picturing them.

> It wad frae monie a blunder free us,
> And foolish notion.

DANCING

DANCING is the oldest art in the world.

It is the primeval form of self-expression.

It is peculiarly the form in which youth shows forth its joy. When grandfather is pleased he smiles. When the boy of six is pleased he jumps up and down, spins about and capers; i. e., dances.

The little lambs leap up, the calves caper, the colts kick and race, the kitten chases its tail, and the puppies indulge in the most twisted antics, all to express their joy in life.

Of human creatures the same is true. Dancing is as natural as singing. It is the first and most satisfactory outlet for the spirit of play.

Is dancing immoral?

Morality consists not in the doing or not doing of this or that. It consists in such a moderate, decent, and intelligent indulgence in any form of pleasure as shall indicate that one is "above his pleasures," always has due regard for the esteem of his world, and never makes his amusement the vehicle for his vices.

One can dance, therefore, quite as morally, as temperately, and self-respectingly as he can dine or sleigh ride.

Dancing is no more moral or immoral than pussy-wants-a-corner or drop-the-handkerchief.

It is not the thunders of the Puritanic moralist that dancing needs; it is the spirit of the gentleman and gentlewoman.

Within the last few years dancing has advanced into an amazing vogue. The so-called "new dances" are such that elderly people can participate in them, as they are simpler and more readily learned than the waltzes, schottisches, and polkas of a former day.

The result has been that instead of sitting about all evening after dinner, smoking, drinking, and playing cards, the older persons arise and shake their legs even as the youth.

Of course there is danger in dancing. There is danger in every kind of self-expression in joy. But the morals of the American people are not going to be corrupted.

The intelligence, good sense, and self-restraint of decent people can be trusted. And if not, then no amount of police control and moral admonition will do them any good.

Whatever induces the people to play more and drink and lounge less is helpful. And dancing is the original play. It is the first impulse of a happy heart in a sound body.

Instead of abolishing dancing in restaurants, we ought to teach it in the public schools.

THE POND OF VANOISE

At Romille, near Fougeres, in France, there is a pretty pond, the pond of the Vanoise it is called.

From twenty leagues around they used to come there to drown themselves, says the Paris *Figaro*. The pond of the Vanoise attracted the candidates for suicide, as if its placid waters exercised an evil spell. In vain the place was watched. Every day or so a body was found.

The inhabitants of Romille, calm Bretons who love life, strongly disapproved of this use of their pond as an extinguisher of vital sparks. They had a meeting, they passed resolutions, they made a motion and took a vote. It was carried. On the banks of the pool they put up signs:

"Defense de se noyer sous peine d'amende." Which may be translated, "Drowning one's self is prohibited under penalty of law."

And the beauty of it is that, since these placards have been placed, no one has dared drown himself in the pond of the Vanoise.

The simplicity and effectiveness of this plan commend it as suitable for universal adoption. At one Alexandrian stroke any civic or social Gordian knot may be loosed.

Are we tired of political bosses, lobbyists, and corruptionists? Simply pass a law that such persons be hereby forbidden to practise their arts and are ordered to go to farming.

Why trifle longer with burglary, arson, and murder? Be it resolved that such offenses be from now on prohibited. And there you are. It is like Columbus and the egg. So simple you never thought of it.

Are we aweary of the strife of opinion? Let us legislate that all people shall, beginning the first of January, be required to think as we think. Then shall we lapse into summer calm and none shall any more argue.

Why be offended further by the drinking of alcoholic liquor, by the use of tobacco, by the end-seat hog, by the slit skirt, by the X-ray robe, by peroxide hair, by crowded street cars, by delayed railway trains, by political parties that do not fulfil their pledges, by gum-chewing and bad grammar?

Let the legislature or city council simply print a number of placards and insert properly paid notices in the newspapers.

"Defense to do any of these things sous peine d'amende."

Just a simple twist of the wrist. The millennium is right here in a minute.

A WONDERFUL SINNER

You have doubtless read that recent story of the woman who lived for seven years in the back office of a lawyer because she loved him and could only love him unlawfully; lived in her mean quarters as a prisoner in a cell, just to be near him, foregoing all the world for him, until one day he died suddenly in her arms, and all their secret joy perished in a moment of shame and death.

This news item lay like a red splash across the page. Among the other news, all of sordid interest, political self-seeking, the snarl of money-monsters, the yelp of taken criminals, the gestures of despair, the preening of society, the vanities of kings, the rumors of war, the long roll of accidents, among all this mud of the ordinary bloomed one morning this story of purple passion, through the coarse clay of events swept this sudden fire of unbelievable love.

I am not going to praise this woman, lest the army of the righteous sweep down on me, lest all the holy hands of those whose secret sins have never bloomed in public be raised to condemn me as a corrupter of public morals.

If they say her sin is great, and that her example is evil and in nowise to be commended or followed, and that it is all a disgraceful, pitiable tale, and one to be suppressed, hushed, and turned away from, and inimical to morals, I have nothing to answer, I cannot defend her.

The woman was a sinner. But I, for one, take off my hat and stand bowed with a great awe before her, for her sin was a love so mighty and strange and unbelievable that beside it most of the comfortable righteousness of the world looks shrunken and little.

When I think of those long days of loneliness gladly spent for a few words of affection, of those intolerable convict hours borne with transfiguring loyalty for the sake of being near the man she adored, I seem to be in the presence of the elemental woman heart, majestic as the high mountains, awful as Niagara or the roar of the storm-driven ocean.

She loved. Where in the pages of romance is to be found such love! Before it our smug conventions are shattered, our nice respectabilities are shrivelled away, our bitter words of condemnation dry upon our lips, and we go out from where she and her Judge stand face to face, as the Pharisees went out from the presence of the Master and the wayward woman when He said: "Neither do I condemn thee. Go and sin no more."

To how many who have read her story has

there come an amazing revelation of the depth, the height, the length, the breadth of that most abysmal of things, a woman's heart! And how many of us, while we talked lightly and carefully of the scandal of it, and said, "It was too bad," have felt in our hearts shamed and belittled, for that we knew that in us was capability of no such greatness, such towering self-sacrifice, no, not even in sin. For even in our sins we are so petty!

MANDRAKES AND MODERNISM

THERE is a vast deal of the world's learning that is pure waste.

I have seen libraries in Europe, books of precious vellum, hand printed, many of them by the lifetime labor of anchorites, and not one of them containing an ounce of wisdom useful today.

Many of our public and private book collections at the present time are for the most part junk heaps.

The worship of books has become a blind cult. We esteem any aggregation of bound volumes a mark of learning.

As a matter of fact, perhaps nine-tenths of the knowledge men accumulated up to a hundred years ago is useless, except to show how much is not worth while.

As a sample of the amazing non-facts men swallowed whole on the word of savants, take the literature of the mandrake.

This plant, the mandragora officinalis of the Mediterranean region, was from the most ancient times endowed by superstition with strange powers. Read the story of Leah's mandrakes in the thirtieth chapter of Genesis.

The reason for the crazy beliefs that attached themselves to this plant was doubtless the shape of its root, which is forked and crudely resembles human legs. The upper part is not unlike a man's body, and with a little skill one can cut the top to look like a head, while if grains are imbedded in the crown they will sprout and give a fair imitation of hair.

Here are some of the "facts":

The mandrake can be used as the basis of a love philter. It will also cure childlessness.

When pulled from the ground it utters a human cry, as in Longfellow's "Spanish Student":

> Teach me where that wondrous mandrake grows,
> Whose magic root, torn from the earth with groans
> At midnight hour, can scare the fiends away
> And make the mind prolific in its fancies.

To uproot a mandrake was dangerous business. Pliny advised first drawing three concentric circles around it with a sword. Theophrastus recommended jumping three times around it. The approved method in the middle ages was to tie a hungry dog to the plant and offer him a piece of meat; he gives a lunge, and there you are! No one hurt with a curse except a dog.

Greek, Latin, and Arabic literature abound in mandrake information. The plant was an intermediate creation between the vegetable and animal kingdoms, as the ape comes between animal and man.

The mandrake is part demon in its powers, part plant in nature, and part human in form.

It doubles the treasure of those who own it.

It knows the future. Ask it a question and it shakes its head.

Boccaccio and Machiavelli, La Fontaine and Caliban make use of it in drama and story.

The best mandrakes are those pulled under a gibbet where hangs a fresh corpse.

Mandrake leaves shine like stars.

All this may serve to show the method of minds before the modern era.

People did not want to know what was true, but what was interesting.

Historical truth is a modern discovery. Scientific truth had no particular value up to a few generations ago.

People then were children, with all a child's credulity, a fact no book has brought out so vividly as Mark Twain's "A Yankee at King Arthur's Court."

The tendency to-day is to accept learned men's statements for nothing, except they be proved. No authority goes. The most famous scientist in the world would be laughed at if he wrote a book of assertions without facts to back them up.

Furthermore, the learned are learning that their sayings have little weight unless they can strip them of long words and technical terms and put them into plain English, understandable of the people.

The wonderful eighteenth and nineteenth centuries saw more than the downfall of the irrational tyranny in government; they saw the beginning of the downfall of all humbug authority in every realm of thought—the first step in the emancipation of mankind.

NEW YEAR'S RESOLUTIONS

THE New Year is here. It is inventory time. Let us look over the stock of habits, ideas, and relationships we have accumulated the past twelve months and clean up.

The New Year's resolution is a good thing. Why drift along, the slave and plaything of our unmanaged desires and of our accidental circumstances? Why not be our own master and live one year like an intelligent human being?

Examine your habits. Lop off the bad ones. Free yourself from any ways you have fallen into that make you lazy, unhealthy, miserable, and disagreeable to other people.

Determine this year to be master of self; that you will control your thoughts, regulate your passions, and guide your own deeds; that you will not let events lead you by the nose.

Resolve to be happy. Remember Lincoln's saying that "folks are usually about as happy as they make up their minds to be."

This year you shall not neglect your friends. They are too valuable, as life assets, to lose.

You will adopt some system and stick to it, knowing that nine-tenths of our irritation comes from lack of system.

Lay out a course of study. No one is too old to learn. Resolve to give some time each day to reading some helpful book. Cut out the trash.

Resolve to keep an account of all the money you get and of all you spend. You may have tried this many times and failed. Never mind; you are still alive and have the chance to try it again.

Save. Put a certain fraction by of all you make. There's no friend like money in the bank.

Don't spend any money till you get it. Don't go into debt. Beware of buying all those things you "must have," for you mustn't have anything until you can pay for it.

No alcohol this year. Let your body rest 365 days from this poison and see how you feel. Don't get into a moral fever over this. Don't "try" not to drink. Just don't drink.

Resolve to take that daily exercise.

Eliminate worry. This year make up your mind to fret over nothing. Adjust yourself to facts instead of getting into a stew over them. If a matter can be helped, help it; if it cannot be helped, forget it.

This year resolve to keep discord out of the house. Nobody can quarrel with you if you do not quarrel with him. Say to yourself that you will not once in 1916 speak crossly to your children; that you will not say one unkind word to your husband or wife, and that you will keep agreeable if it takes a leg.

This may be the last year you will have. Make it a good one.

You know how you ought to live. At least, you think you do. And if you do as well as your own judgment tells you, it will be an advance.

This is old-fashioned advice. But happiness is old-fashioned, and life. There is no new-fangled way to be content.

And learn this of wise Marcus Aurelius:

"To change thy mind and follow him that sets thee right is to be none the less the free agent that thou wast before."

Also: "The happiness and unhappiness of the rational social animal depends not on what he feels but on what he does; just as virtue and vice consist not in feeling but in doing."

AN OPEN LETTER TO SANTA CLAUS

MY DEAR SANTA CLAUS: I am writing to you in behalf of the several millions of people in this country who are orthodox.

By orthodox I mean those who believe in you. We also believe in fairies and angels. We believe that the spirits of dead mothers still are near to all little boys and girls, and love them always, and look after them, and often put good thoughts into their minds, and kiss them in their sleep. And that fathers who are dead are living yet and loving their children and working for them somewhere.

We believe in you, dear Santa Claus, because you do not do anything else but come around once a year and make children happy. Surely anybody who is in that business ought to be believed in, whether he exists or not.

But you do exist. You live in the hearts and fancies of thousands and thousands of little people, and surely that is a much better place to live than in a big house in a fine city.

So, when you come dashing along with your reindeer and your sledful of toys on Christmas Eve, don't forget that many, many eager eyes are upon you and a vast number of little hearts are fluttering in tune and time with your sleighbells.

Our stockings will be hung up, as usual, around the fireplace. If we haven't a fireplace you can find them hung up on the radiator or the back of a chair. For we know that people who build houses without fireplaces cannot fool you, and that you can come down the steam pipe or creep in through the keyhole just as easily as you used to enter houses by chimneys.

Please don't bring us useful presents, like mittens and handkerchiefs. We want red wagons and dolls, and all sorts of those funny and Christmasy thingumajigs that you know so well how to make. Also please bring some striped stick candy, because we can suck it a long time and it doesn't give us the stomach ache.

If you see a very tiny stocking hanging among the others, don't overlook it. That's the baby's. He is not old enough, of course, to know what Christmas means, but go on, put something in his stocking anyhow, because we don't want him left out. Please do this.

And don't forget grandma's stocking. She doesn't want to hang it up, but we are going to make her, because she is the very sweetest, darlingest grandma in all the whole world, and she believes in you, and has told us lots about you. Haven't you any grandma toys?

We are all going to bed early and sleep tight as tight can be on Christmas Eve, and we promise honestly not to look, and we will be up early Christmas morning; so be sure and come.

And please, please don't forget the poor children. You know it takes only the cheapest kind of a toy to make them happy, to make them know that Christmas is really and truly here.

So come, dear old Santa Claus, come to the myriad children who adore you, to the mother hearts that live again their childhood days when you visit them, to the fathers who, when they hear you coming, are changed "and become as little children," and even to all those whose babies are no more about them, but are gone to live with the blessed dead.

We need you; and this world would be poorer and so waste and sad if you and the fairies and the angels should lose faith in us and come no more.

P. S.—Last night little Tim, when he was saying his prayers, said "God bless Santa Claus, too." So you see there's one little fellow in this house that thinks you're all right.

SHAKESPEARE

Back to Shakespeare!

Study him in your youth, and in your old age he will come back to comfort you.

If you would be a writer, learn from him how grandeur of thought can flow in a limpid style, and how an exquisite judgment can choose the one word wherein trembles the essence of conviction.

If you would speak in public, let him be your master in that combined conciseness and eloquence that warms men's hearts while it persuades their minds.

If you would know human nature and grasp the art of living, make familiar friends of his characters, high and low, mean and noble, and you shall come into that universality of experience no man than he has better set forth.

Of all Time's figures he appears the most amazing. The empires of Napoleon and Charlemagne have dissolved. The books of poets, essayists, and novelists who have been acclaimed by the people as immortal have stood awhile, and at last have fallen from their pedestals, but Shakespeare remains, polished and perfect, the admiration of present day intelligence as much as when Ben Jonson sang his praise.

He has been attacked and derided, his flaws have been pointed out. His very existence has been denied. But all the waves of criticism have beaten in vain upon the edifice of his fame. He remains to-day the greatest master of the greatest language of history. There is no other author where you can find English in its ideal perfection.

He is a true master of men. As has been said: "What king has he not taught state? What maiden has not found him finer than her delicacy? What lover has he not outloved? What gentleman has he not instructed in the rudeness of his behavior?"

Read your Shakespeare, young men and women! If he bores you, it is for the same reason that the noble bores the low and narrow; read on, until you catch step with that majestical mind; read on, and find your littleness falling from you and your soul growing great!

And rest assured that it is a sad thing for us when we cannot have a whole-souled admiration for those real kings of men whom Time has tested and all mankind has crowned.

Buy the small editions of his separate plays. Carry a little volume in your pocket. Pencil it. Read, mark, learn, and inwardly digest. Read aloud his sounding phrases to another or to yourself. Commit to memory those lines which find you.

The mind to whom Shakespeare is a constant companion cannot be entirely commonplace; for in Shakespeare is the soul of the English race at its best.

THE ANONYMOUS LETTER

LIFT up your hand right now and swear that never, so long as you live, and so help you God, will you write an anonymous letter, except it be a kind one. After which please kiss the Bible.

If you hate anybody, either go and whip him, or else go away and let him alone.

Don't stab him in the back, don't put poison in his tea, don't shoot him from behind a fence corner, and, what is worse, because still more cowardly, don't write him an anonymous letter.

The anonymous letter is the triumph of the petty. It is the victory of the impotent. It is the pride of the cowardly.

The writer of such a letter is a copperhead snake, which differs from the gentlemanly rattlesnake in that it strikes without warning.

An open, out and out enemy who loathes you heartily and says so is a wholesome person. He keeps you humble and makes you careful. But the man that smiles on you and goes home and writes you an anonymous letter is too low to be described here, on account of the postal laws.

Of course you do not use profane language, which is naughty. But recall all the bad words you ever heard, the unrepeatable vile epithets of all the languages you know, focus them upon one point—that is the anonymous letter writer.

Don't hint. Don't insinuate. Insult if you must, but do it in plain English. And sign your name.

Imitate the clerk, who was called to the boss's office. The boss said:

"Mr. Brown, I understand you have been making insinuations about me."

"Oh, no. That must be a mistake."

"It is no mistake, Mr. Brown. I have it upon the best authority. Don't try to wriggle out of it."

"But it must be a mistake. I never insinuate. To be sure, I said you were an old muttonhead and a rascal, but I never insinuated anything."

By common consent, since the world was built, and men began the great game of fighting each other for gold, for woman, and for nothing at all, the sneak, the spy, and the traitor have been blackballed from the society of brave men. Away down below sneak, spy, and traitor in the list of human detestables may be found the man or woman who enjoys sending an anonymous letter.

If you are full of venom and must get it out of your system write—write fully and foully. Then burn your letter. Thus it may relieve yourself and hurt no one.

GOLDEN ROD

It has come, the army with golden plumes, and conquered the land.

Every wall is held, every highway is sentinelled. There are squadrons in the meadows and pickets in the woods.

So quietly the little soldiers came, myriads upon myriads of them, stealing northward by moonlight, spreading east and west guided by the winds and piped to by the birds in the hedgerows, so gently were we beleaguered, that until but a few days ago we knew it not, and then when we strolled far out one Sunday in the countryside we saw them, sheen of pure gold in the sun, nodding clusters of the most beautiful royal yellow in the world, happy groups laughing to us from the wayside, until we were all atremble with the exquisiteness, the daintiness, the consummate wonder of it all, and "or ever I was aware my soul made me like the chariots of the Aminadab."

There are other flowers for other spirit moods, for other seasons. We must love the little crocus, first born of the sun and the woman-earth, as it thrusts its fragile beauty up through the snow upon the warm side of the house; and the violet, shy beneath its covering leaf, blue as a speck of sky fallen timid and chaste; and the brilliant dandelions, smearing the grass fields as with a brush dipped in the sun; and the wild roses, like sweet thoughts of young girls gladdening the dusty road; and hollyhocks and marigold, pinks and forget-me-nots, roses and rue; but what can compare with this gypsy flower of the open, this flower uncultured and unimprovable by man, the direct gift and most gracious handiwork of God, the Master Craftsman of beauty, who lends the earth, at the death of summer, this garment of cloth-of-gold as a splendid cerement!

Lovers love you, little Golden Rod. I saw them wandering in the woodland and along the lanes, gathering armfuls of your treasure.

Mothers love you and set you in their windows to catch the sun.

And I know a man (and how many are there, brothers of his spirit?) who goes out alone and looks at you these days, and finds your charm singing in his heart, a broken heart that seems to mend in your presence, for he thinks of her who last year walked beside him, as glorious in her eyes and smile as you are glorious, and who loved you so, and he takes the fullest and richest of your blooms, and lays them on the little mound where she sleeps forever.

You too must go, Golden Rod, as all beauty must go, for evanescence is writ on earthly joy. But would you might stay always with us,

> Clothing the palpable and familiar
> With golden exhalations of the dawn.